NEXT STEPS FOR THE 1980s IN STUDENT FINANCIAL AID

A Fourth Alternative

*Comments and Recommendations
by the Carnegie Council
on Policy Studies
in Higher Education*

NEXT STEPS FOR THE 1980s IN STUDENT FINANCIAL AID

A Fourth Alternative

Jossey-Bass Publishers

San Francisco • Washington • London • 1979

NEXT STEPS FOR THE 1980s IN STUDENT FINANCIAL AID
A Fourth Alternative
    The Carnegie Council on Policy Studies in Higher Education

The Carnegie Council Series

The following technical reports are available from the Carnegie
Council on Policy Studies in Higher Education, 2150 Shattuck Avenue,
Berkeley, California 94704.

Contents

*The federal guarantee • The problem of
tracing borrowers • The scarcity of loan
funds • The problem of repayment •
Interest subsidies • The pattern of
proliferating complexity • The National
Direct Student Loan program • Fundamental
problems of both programs • Tinkering
versus thorough reform • A National Student
Loan Bank • Fundamental choices*

*The varied situations of part-time students •
General rules for part-time students •
Independent students*

*Coordination by packaging • Political
coordination • Federal and state
responsibilities • Program complementarity •
Coordination and self-help expectations •
Coordination by covering specific expenses •
Federal support for state scholarship
programs • Sharing the burden*

*The essential commitments • The conditions
of meeting these essential commitments •
The necessary burdens • Reconciling other*

Preface

Financial aid to students for the sake of equalizing opportunity for access to higher education has been a long-time concern of the Carnegie Council on Policy Studies in Higher Education and of the Carnegie Commission on Higher Education before it.[1]

The Congress and the federal administration are preparing for a reexamination of the financial aid system in advance of the expected legislation on the Higher Education Amendments of 1979; or, possibly, of 1980. This report is intended to be helpful to this reexamination and to the prior consideration of policy options by the higher education community.

The Council expresses its appreciation to Margaret S. Gordon and to Martin Kramer for their assistance.

---

[1]See Carnegie Commission on Higher Education, *Quality and Equality: New Levels of Federal Responsibility for Higher Education* (1968); *Quality and Equality: Revised Recommendations—New Levels of Federal Responsibility for Higher Education* (1970); *Institutional Aid: Federal Support to Colleges and Universities* (1972); and *Higher Education: Who Pays? Who Benefits? Who Should Pay?* (1973). See also Carnegie Council on Policy Studies in Higher Education, *The Federal Role in Postsecondary Education: Unfinished Business 1975-1980* (1975); The Carnegie Foundation for the Advancement of Teaching, *The States and Higher Education: A Proud Past and a Vital Future* (1976); and Carnegie Council on Policy Studies in Higher Education, *The States and Private Higher Education: Problems and Policies in a New Era* (1977).

NEXT STEPS FOR THE 1980s IN STUDENT FINANCIAL AID

A Fourth Alternative

Part One

Making Better Use
of Existing Resources

1

General Comments: Doing More with No More Money

In 1979 the Congress and the administration will consider legislation to extend and revise the Higher Education Act, and, in the process, will review the structure of the student aid system. These considerations may extend into 1980.

At least three alternatives are likely to be discussed. We add, in this report, a fourth.

The three likely alternatives are:

1. A simple extension of existing legislation with no, or only minor, changes
2. A further expansion of the "middle-income" thrust that animated the 1978 legislation, carrying aid programs in larger amounts and to higher levels of family income to students whose families are located in the upper half of the income range
3. A renewed effort to add (and perhaps eventually to substitute) a program of cost-of-education tax credits

The additional alternative we strongly recommend involves:

4. A major overhaul of the existing package of programs to make them more equitable in their impact and more sound

in their administration—within the confines of about the same cost to the federal and state governments combined.

The surrounding situation for the new debate over student aid includes, among many other important elements, the following:

A federal government under contrary pressures:

- To hold down expenditures, including in the student aid area where they have increased substantially—by 600 percent in the past 10 years in money terms and 300 percent in constant dollars—in recent years
- To respond, simultaneously, to the continuing demands of "middle-income" parents for selective relief, which strongly affected the 1978 adjustments via additional student aid or via tax credits

State governments highly conscious of Proposition 13 sentiment in their districts and hesitant about raising expenditures for higher education and for other social programs.

Colleges and universities fearful of the future under the additive pressures of potentially declining enrollments, continuing inflation that hits them very hard, and the growing hesitancy of many states to augment their support. A corollary of this is an intensified conflict between public and private, and two-year and four-year institutions over their respective shares of public aid.

Under these circumstances, what, of a constructive nature might best be done?

Where We Now Stand

We would like to note very briefly in advance some of the accomplishments of the student aid program to date upon which we seek to build:

1. Women and members of minority groups from families with incomes below the median have increased their enrollment rates substantially since the introduction of the Basic Grant program in 1972—by 22 percent to the academic year 1976-77, from an absolute rate of 12.4 percent to a rate of 15.1 percent, involving 240,000 persons (this figure may rise to 300,000 by 1979-80 on the basis of our estimates). Some of this increase may also be ascribed to affirmative action, to the spread of low-cost community colleges, to inadequate job opportunities for young persons in a period of depression and recession, to the availability of educational aid to veterans, and to the general temper of the times when more young people have sought to widen their range of opportunities and have been encouraged to do so by their families. Yet much of the 22 percent increase in rates of enrollment can be credited to the greatly increased availability of student aid. About 12 percent of the expenditures on Basic Grants in 1976-77 may be attributed to the cost of this expansion of opportunity. The percentage is less than 12 when calculated against all student aid programs, and also when it is calculated on the basis of Basic Grants alone after the 1978 changes that targeted more money on the upper-middle-income group;[1] almost certainly less than 10 percent in all. It should be noted, parenthetically, that attendance rates of white males have gone down during this period, chiefly because of the end of the military draft; but they might have gone down even more without the availability of additional student aid.

2. Public student aid funds have enabled many private colleges with limited resources of their own to recruit and serve more low-income students. Enrollments as a whole have been

---

[1]We define *upper-middle income* as the second highest quartile in the income range (see Table 5 in the Glossary). In popular parlance, this has been *middle income*. The 1978 changes added students from this income range (roughly 22 percent of all students) to those from the lower half of the income range (roughly 27 percent of all students) as eligible for need-based federal aid.

somewhat higher than they otherwise might have been. Induced enrollments for men and women and for majority and minority students combined have probably amounted to about 5 percent more than they otherwise might have been. Individual institutions have benefited in enrollment gains to quite diverse degrees—some substantially, some little or not at all.

3. Parents have been relieved of many sacrifices that sending a child to college traditionally entails for all but the wealthy. This reduction of the burden on parents was greatly accelerated by the 1978 amendments. The bulk of student aid funds, now totaling about $6 billion (not counting veterans' educational benefits) and certainly more than half and possibly two thirds, has gone to reduce the burden on parents whose children, whether there had been any new student aid programs or not, would have gone to college. Before the 1978 amendments this parental relief was concentrated on the lower half of the income range; now it is concentrated on the lower three quarters. More of the cost of college attendance, in part because of the new student aid programs, is now borne by public agencies and less by individuals. The family share of the total costs of higher education has fallen from about 40 to 30 percent over the past decade; the public share has risen from 50 to 60 percent; and the philanthropic share has remained even at about 10 percent. Student aid is now 90 percent from public sources, as compared with 65 percent ten years ago; it was nearly zero percent from public sources before World War II.

4. We find no evidence that colleges generally have raised tuition levels above what they otherwise would have been because of the additional student aid, although some have undoubtedly done so. Tuition levels have risen at about their historic rates, including adjustment for inflation; not faster.

5. We find no conclusive evidence that students work less than before—although inconclusive evidence indicates there may have been a drop over the past decade for students from lower-income families; but the average standard of living of students has increased as it has for the population as a whole.

The Fourth Alternative

We propose an alternative that has the following components:

- No increase in the total amount spent on student aid by the federal government
- A redistribution of funds in the direction of what we consider to be the greater needs
- A better coordination of federal and state programs, with greater incentives for increased state expenditures
- Changes that will add to the integrity, and to the simplicity and flexibility, of the overall program.

We will return to these four considerations at the end of this section.

We see the following specific opportunities for improvement within the context of political and economic realities:

- The introduction of an explicit self-help component (through earnings but also through borrowing) by the students themselves
- A loan system that makes loans more easily and widely available and at much less risk of heavy default rates
- Additional assurances of equality of opportunity for all young persons to obtain a college education if they wish—this has been and continues to be our first priority
- A greater range of choice for students and potential students

Each of these opportunities for improvement will be discussed, in order, below. They are set forth as specific recommendations in Section 2.

An Explicit Self-Help Component

We propose that the basic building block of student financial support for postsecondary education be a substantial self-help component. We do this for the following reasons:

- Family income is no longer a sufficient indication of need, both because of the high and increasing proportion of students listing themselves as "independent," some of whom are really independent and some of whom find this description a way to maximize public support; and because aid is now given to students whose families are in the upper half of the income range and who would go to college whether public aid were available or not—they clearly do not have "need" so critical that, were this need unmet, they could not attend any college. Family income levels distinguish students less and less by degree of real need for available student aid funds.

Self-help, in any event, is intrinsically a better indication of both a student's need for support and of his or her determination to secure a higher education. What effort is the student willing to make to finance his or her further education? Such self-help is in the long-standing American tradition of self-reliance, and it gives assurance to the public at large that governmental aid has been merited by individual effort and not just by manipulation of the rules or by political pressure. Additionally, we believe that an explicit self-help component is an important aspect of developing in students a sense of responsibility for their own advancement and of encouraging a more acutely sensed necessity for prudent use of time and money.

We suggest that the basic self-help component for lower-division students be $600 and for upper-division students be $1,000 per year by 1982-83. This would require 180 hours of work per year (or some combination of work and loans) at the lower-division level. This could be accomplished by a little more than half a day (5 hours) a week during the academic year at the minimum wage rate that is scheduled to go to $3.35 per hour in 1981; or by a little more than two months (9 weeks) of work in the summer, including time to earn subsistence expenses for the summer months; or by some combination of the two. At the upper-division level, this would amount to just over a day (8.33 hours) a week during the academic year; or less than 3 months (12 weeks) in the summer; or some combination of the two. We note that upper-division students, in particular, are likely to be paid above the minimum rate, thus reducing the number of required hours.

We consider these amounts of work quite reasonable. About 40 percent of all students in 1975-76 had summer employment and earned an average of about $700; and 40 percent had termtime employment and earned about $1,200. The proportion of all students who have both or only one of these sources of income is unknown; but we estimate that perhaps two thirds of all students work either in summer or during termtime or both. Also, in the 1980s, with a substantially reduced age cohort, job opportunities for young persons should be greatly improved.

We are convinced that reasonable amounts of work, perhaps to a maximum of 20 hours a week, are not only possible but also desirable. It has been found that work during termtime up to 20 hours a week is positively correlated with persistence of students in school. Work builds social ties to the campus and to the community. It also provides work experience for the employment record of students and as a source of recommendations.

We also suggest an additional $200 self-help expectation per student prior to receipt of an allowance under the State Student Incentive Grant (SSIG) program.

In lieu of work, students may wish to substitute loans in whole or in part.

We note that, in the longer run, as more and more students become "independent," and as levels of eligibility for aid creep higher and higher in the family income range, as they have done so dramatically over the past decade, public policy will be driven either toward across-the-board aid to all students, which would be both very expensive and very unnecessary, or to some explicit reliance on self-help. We strongly prefer the latter of these two courses of development. Any self-help component will, of course, need to be adjusted over time to rising levels of earnings and of costs of attending college. Experience with it should be carefully monitored to be sure that it is not interfering with academic endeavors.

A Better Long-Term Loan System

We propose, once again, the creation of a National Student Loan Bank. This bank would be largely self-sufficient. It would make loans available toward meeting college costs to students without any proof of their being needy, with payments possible over an extended period of time. Under our proposal, loans would be used mainly under these three circumstances: a student could work but prefers not to do so; parents could pay, but either do not wish to do so or the student does not wish to call upon them to do so; or the student wants to attend a higher-cost institution. Loans would not be a question of necessity; they would, rather, add to the range of choices available.

We consider current default rates under the present program to be quite beyond reason, although we applaud the progress being made by the Office of Education in reducing them. Some of the specific default rates have been scandalous.

More Equality of Opportunity for Low-Income Students

Low-income students can now receive, through the Basic Grant programs, not over one half of the cost of attending college. The 50 percent rule was strictly a political compromise. We suggest abandoning this rule and substituting the self-help component. Under our proposed formula, the self-help component would result in a maximum Basic Grant award equal to about 70 percent of full cost for lower-division students and about 55 percent for upper-division students at a comparatively low-cost institution. Thus, students in full need would be guaranteed, as was the intent of the original legislation, the minimum financial capability of attending some college through the combination of self-help and Basic Grants. We consider this to be the most urgent priority.

Not all students can easily find work on campus. We suggest a major expansion of the College Work-Study (CWS) program. It will help students meet the self-help component. It also helps institutions meet their costs of operation. To serve its purposes, CWS should give some preference to students attending colleges in high unemployment areas and in rural areas, and to women students—many of whom have a harder time than men finding jobs and, when they do so, only at lower rates of pay. The average earnings from CWS for those with CWS support is now $650 a year and will be $800 a year in 1981 if average pay rates rise with the increase in the federal minimum wage.

We also propose an override to each institution of 10 percent of the amount of Basic Grants received on campus to take care of special situations, at the discretion of the institution, provided the money is spent only for the general purposes intended. This would help take care (1) of handicapped persons who cannot work, (2) of those students who can work but cannot find any or adequate employment, (3) of those who can work but must spend extra class time making up academic deficiencies, (4) of those who are in real need but cannot get a Basic Grant because they are registered for less than half-time study, (5) of those who have minor dependents without other adequate sources of support, and (6) of those below the age of 18 who may not be required to meet the self-help expectation. In each of these situations, individual students could receive up to 100 percent of the Basic Grant allowance. This would allow for situations where students, for reasons beyond their control, cannot meet in full or even at all the self-help component or where they otherwise have special needs. We propose that the maximum Basic Grant rise from the current $1,800 to $2,400 by 1982-83.

These several provisions, along with other changes we suggest, would meet the promise made in 1972 that no young person should be denied the opportunity to attend college for reasons of financial deprivation alone. These changes are set forth at the end of this section.

A Greater Range of Choice for Students

We propose:

- The retention of the Supplemental Educational Opportunity Grant program. The SEOG program provides flexibility in relation to tuition costs similar to that which will be provided by the special 10 percent supplement to Basic Grants according to our suggestion.
- A very major expansion of the State Student Incentive Grant program, with added assurances that federal matching funds be used for students in need.
- A new provision, as part of SSIG, that will encourage the portability of student grants.

• A much improved student loan system, as set forth above.

Each of these, and all of them together, will increase the range of choice of students to attend higher-cost public and private institutions and to go to institutions outside their states of residence.

Additionally, we suggest ways in which part-time students, including adults, can be aided to attend college. In particular, the supplemental 10 percent allowance in the Basic Grant program can help students registered for less than half time.

Earlier we mentioned four general components of our proposed fourth alternative. We should now like to return to them:

• Our program would not increase the total amount spent on student aid programs by the federal government and by the states. The Office of Education (OE) "package" would increase with more money for the Basic Grant, CWS, and SSIG programs, partially offset by less for loan programs. We note that veterans' educational benefits will go down as a matter of course (we estimate a reduction of $1,100 million from 1979-80 to 1982-83; from $1,900 million to $800 million); but we do not think it realistic that this money will be recaptured for other student aid programs—the Department of Defense will probably absorb the reduction into the financing of its programs. However, we propose elimination of Social Security benefits for students and also food stamps, on the grounds that our program will make them unnecessary. These reductions should be calculated against the increase in the OE "package." The SSIG program we propose would cost the states substantial additional funds. This should also be taken into account, and when it is, the total amount spent on student aid by the federal and state governments together will remain roughly what it is now in constant dollars, assuming all the states take full advantage of federal matching funds—it is quite possible that some of them will choose not to do so. Over a period of time, to the extent that enrollments decline in the 1980s and 1990s, there may be expected to be some overall decline in the amounts of student aid in constant dollars. The overall decline in the numbers of young persons, however, will not bring much of a decline in young persons from lower-income families, whose members are rising proportionately within the total youth group.

- The redistribution we suggest would aid low-income students (our first priority) and enhance students' choice (our second priority) in selecting an institution. The latter of these, in particular, will aid in creating fairer competition among institutions (our third priority) based more than now on considerations of the value to students of their academic programs.

- Our several proposals will lead to better coordination of federal and state programs, with the federal government primarily concerned with the subsistence costs of attending college, and the states with adjustments required by their many different combinations of public and private institutions and of tuition policies among public institutions.

- In several ways the overall program would gain: in integrity— by lower default rates on loans, by less tendency artificially to manufacture "independent" status for students, and by the requirement of explicit self-help as a basis for aid; and in simplicity and flexibility by eliminating a need requirement for loans and by adding a 10 percent adjustment to Basic Grants which will both simplify the rules for the distribution of the funds available without this override and more precisely meet individual needs. The SEOG program, which is now in operation and which we recommend be continued, also provides for flexibility in use of funds at the campus level. We also suggest that consideration be given to a "bank-account" approach to student aid so that students could draw only so much of it without exhausting their accounts and becoming no longer eligible; this would encourage students to plan any withdrawals from their accounts more carefully.

We advance this fourth alternative as costing the federal government no more money (see Figure 1 and Table 1) but greatly improving the overall program as compared with the first alternative (extension of existing legislation); as more likely, in the current economic and political climate, than the

Figure 1. Estimated expenditures under existing federal and state student aid programs, 1979-80, and under Carnegie Council recommendations, 1982-83 (in millions of constant—1979—dollars, excluding veterans' educational benefits)[a]

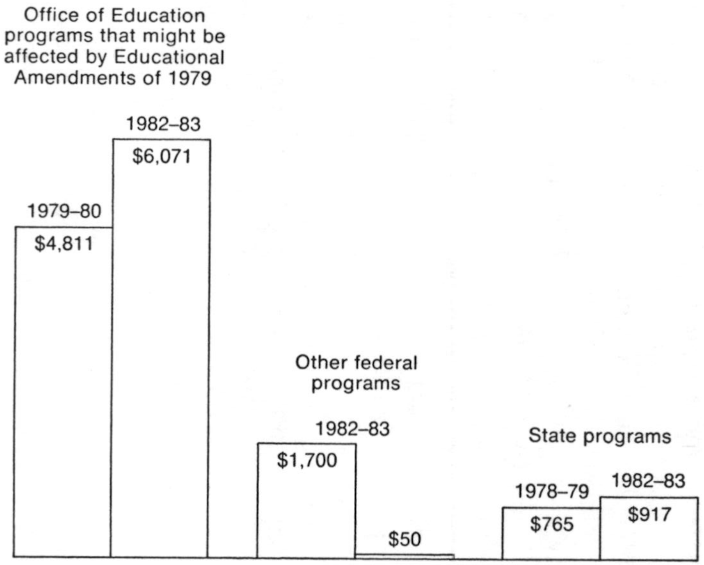

Office of Education programs that might be affected by Educational Amendments of 1979

1982-83
$6,071

1979-80
$4,811

Other federal programs

1982-83
$1,700

$50

State programs

1978-79
$765

1982-83
$917

Suggested changes to 1982-83

Office of Education programs that might be affected by Educational Amendments of 1979

Basic Grants	
Regular program	+$685
Special 10 percent override	+ 324
Supplementary Educational Opportunity Grants	0
College Work-Study program	+ 350
Guaranteed Student Loan program	− 660
National Direct Student Loan program	− 329
State Student Incentive Grant program	+ 840
National Student Loan Bank	+ 50
Total	+ 1,260

Other federal programs

Social security benefits	− 1,550
Food stamp program	− 100
Total	− 1,650

State programs

	+ 152
Grand Total	− 238

[a]Estimates are based on projected 1979-80 enrollment (by family income and cost of institutions); actual enrollment in 1982-83 is likely to differ little in total numbers from that in 1979-80.

Source: Table 1.

Table 1. Estimated expenditures under existing federal and state student aid programs, 1979-80, and under Carnegie Council recommendations, 1982-83 (in millions of constant—1979—dollars, excluding veterans' educational benefits)

Program	1979-80	1982-83	Change, 1979-80 to 1982-83
Office of Education programs that might be affected by Educational Amendments of 1979			
Basic Grants			
Regular program	$2,555[a]	$3,240	+$685
Special 10 percent override	—	324	+ 324
Supplemental Educational Opportunity Grants	340	340	0
College Work-Study program	550	900	+ 350
Guaranteed Student Loan program	960	300[b]	− 660
National Direct Student Loan program	329	0	− 329
State Student Incentive Grant program	77	917	+ 840
National Student Loan Bank	—	50	+ 50
Total	4,811	6,071	+1,260
Other federal programs			
Social security benefits for college students	1,600[c]	50[d]	−1,550
Food Stamp program	100	0	− 100
Total	1,700	50	−1,650
Total federal programs	6,511	6,121	− 390
State programs	(1978-79)		
States that would need to increase appropriations			(+367)
States that could reduce appropriations			(−215)
Total state programs	765	917	+ 152
Grand total	7,276	7,038	− 238

[a]Administration budget figure for 1979-80 plus the estimated cost of raising the family size offset for independent students without dependents.

[b]There would be a residual cost of several hundred million dollars in the Guaranteed Student Loan program for interest subsidies and defaults under outstanding loans.

[c]The estimated cost of $1,600 million to the Old Age Survivor Disability Insurance (OASDI) trust fund in 1982-83 (in 1979 dollars) if social security benefits for college students are continued.

[d]The estimated additional cost to other student aid programs if social security benefits for college students are discontinued. The additional cost would be small because a large proportion of social security beneficiaries receives Basic Grants now, and many more would be eligible under the Middle-Income Student Assistance Act of 1978.

Source: Carnegie Council estimates.

second alternative (a further expansion of the "middle income" thrust) and, in any event, we see no strong argument for such a further thrust either in a deteriorating ability of "middle-income" families to support children in college (see Figure 2), or in traditional tests of adequacy and fairness of parental contributions; and as clearly preferable to the third alternative, which calls for the introduction of tax credits, which are regressive, very costly to the national budget, and of comparatively little help to individual families because of their widespread distribution.

We recognize that our program will have differing impacts on different types of students and institutions.

Selected Impacts of Carnegie Council Recommendations

Students. There will be improved benefits for low-income students if the suggestions of the Council are accepted. They include:

1. *Much more adequate provision for noninstructional costs in Basic Grant programs.* Under Carnegie Council proposals, the lower-division student can receive up to $1,800 for non-instructional costs, or up to $2,400 under special circumstances. Present regulations limit provision for noninstructional costs for a commuting student to $1,500, and this amount can be severely reduced under the 50-percent-of-cost limitation (see the illustrative cases in Table 2). Even the upper-division student, who would normally receive only a $1,400 maximum grant under our proposals, can now sometimes receive considerably less than this under the 50-percent-of-cost limitation.

2. *Substantially larger Basic Grants for students from families with incomes in the $6,000 to $18,000 range,* as a result of the shift to the schedule of the College Scholarship Service and the American College Testing (CSS/ACT) program (see Figure 3).

3. *A more equitable self-help provision that does not penalize the lower-income student attending a low-cost college.* Our proposed self-help expectation would, under normal circumstances, treat all students alike, whereas the existing 50-percent-of-cost limitation discriminates against lower-income students attending low-cost colleges.

Figure 2. Changes in family income before and after taxes, expected parental contribution, college charges, and consumer price index, for average upper-middle-income family and for average lower- to lower-middle-income family,[a] 1967 to 1978

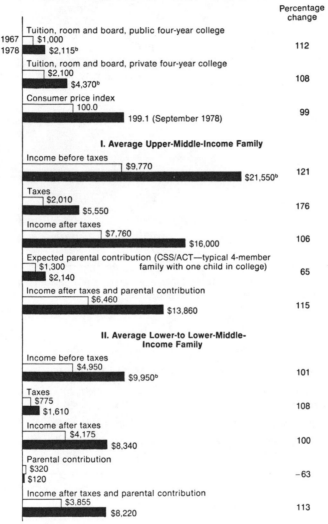

	Percentage change
Tuition, room and board, public four-year college	
1967 $1,000	
1978 $2,115[b]	112
Tuition, room and board, private four-year college	
$2,100	
$4,370[b]	108
Consumer price index	
100.0	
199.1 (September 1978)	99

I. Average Upper-Middle-Income Family

Income before taxes	
$9,770	
$21,550[b]	121
Taxes	
$2,010	
$5,550	176
Income after taxes	
$7,760	
$16,000	106
Expected parental contribution (CSS/ACT—typical 4-member family with one child in college)	
$1,300	
$2,140	65
Income after taxes and parental contribution	
$6,460	
$13,860	115

II. Average Lower-to Lower-Middle-Income Family

Income before taxes	
$4,950	
$9,950[b]	101
Taxes	
$775	
$1,610	108
Income after taxes	
$4,175	
$8,340	100
Parental contribution	
$320	
$120	−63
Income after taxes and parental contribution	
$3,855	
$8,220	113

[a]The average middle-upper-income family is the median family in the next-to-top family income quartile, while the average lower- to lower-middle-income family is a family at the top of the lowest family income quartile. Quartile boundaries are computed from data for all families (see Table 5).

[b]Estimated by projecting on the basis of changes in the years from 1972 to 1977.

Sources: Carnegie Council calculations based on data available from U.S. National Center for Education Statistics; U.S. Bureau of Labor Statistics; U.S. Bureau of the Census; Internal Revenue Service; Social Security Administration; and College Scholarship Service of the College Entrance Examination Board.

Table 2. Comparison of sources of support for typical students under
existing policies and Carnegie Council recommendations, 1982-83
(in 1979 dollars)

	Existing policies	Carnegie Council recommendations	Educational costs	

1. Lower-income student attending low-cost community college as commuter. Family income = $6,000.

	Existing policies	Carnegie Council recommendations	Educational costs	
Basic Grant	$ 850	$1,800	Tuition	$ 200
			Other	2,400
			Total	2,600
Parental contribution	0	0		
Tuition grant (only in certain states at present)	200	0		
Explicit self-help expectation	500[a]	800		
Residual to be met from other sources[b]	1,050 to 1,750	0		

2. Lower-income student attending moderate-cost public four-year college as resident, lower division. Family income = $6,000.

	Existing policies	Carnegie Council recommendations	Educational costs	
Basic Grant	$1,575	$1,800	Tuition	$ 650
			Other	2,500
			Total	3,150
Parental contribution	0	0		
Tuition grant (only certain states at present)	650	400		
Explicit self-help expectation	500[a]	850		
Residual to be met from other sources[b]	425 to 1,575	100		

3. Lower-income student attending high-cost private four-year college as resident, lower-division. Family income = $6,000. [c]

	Existing policies	Carnegie Council recommendations	Educational costs	
Basic Grant	$1,800	$1,800	Tuition	$3,820
			Other	2,900
			Total	6,720
Parental contribution	0	0		
Tuition grant (only certain states at present)	1,500	1,500		

Table 2

	Existing policies	Carnegie Council recommen- dations	Educational costs	
Explicit self-help expectation	$ 500[a]	$ 850		
Residual to be met from other sources[b]	2,920 to 4,920	2,570		

4. Lower-middle-income student attending low-cost community college as commuter. Family income = $15,000.

Basic Grant	$ 850	$1,256	Tuition	$ 200
			Other	2,400
			Total	2,600
Parental contribution	717	544		
Tuition grant (only in certain states at present)	200	0		
Explicit self-help expectation	500[a]	800		
Residual to be met from other sources[b]	333 to 1,033	0		

5. Lower-middle-income student attending moderate-cost public four-year college as resident, lower division. Family income = $15,000.

Basic Grant	$1,083	$1,256	Tuition	$ 650
			Other	2,500
			Total	3,150
Parental contribution	717	544		
Tuition grant (only in certain states at present)	650	400		
Explicit self-help expectation	500[a]	850		
Residual to be met from other sources[b]	200 to 1,350	100		

6. Lower-middle-income student attending high-cost private four-year college as resident, lower division. Family income = $15,000.

Basic Grant	$1,083	$1,256	Tuition	$3,820
			Other	2,900
			Total	6,720

(continued on next page)

Table 2 *(continued)*

	Existing policies	Carnegie Council recommendations	Educational costs
Parental contribution	$ 717	$ 544	
Tuition grant (only in certain states at present)	1,500	1,500	
Explicit self-help expectation	500[a]	850	
Residual to be met from other sources[b]	2,920 to 4,920	2,570	

7. Upper-middle-income student attending low-cost community college as commuter. Family income = $23,000.

	Existing policies	Carnegie Council recommendations	Educational costs	
Basic Grant	$ 229	$ 229	Tuition	$ 200
			Other	2,400
			Total	2,600
Parental contribution	1,571	1,571		
Tuition grant (only in certain states at present)	200	0		
Explicit self-help expectation	500[a]	800		
Residual to be met from other sources[b]	100 to 800	0		

8. Upper-middle-income student attending moderate-cost public four-year college as resident, lower-division. Family income = $23,000.

	Existing policies	Carnegie Council recommendations	Educational costs	
Basic Grant	$ 229	$ 229	Tuition	$ 650
			Other	2,500
			Total	3,150
Parental contribution	1,571	1,571		
Tuition grant (only in certain states at present)	650	400		
Explicit self-help expectation	500[a]	850		
Residual to be met from other sources[b]	200 to 1,350	100		

Table 2

	Existing policies	Carnegie Council recommen-dations	Educational costs	

9. Upper-middle-income student attending high-cost private four-year college as resident, lower-division. Family income = $23,000.

	Existing policies	Carnegie Council recommendations	Educational costs	
Basic Grant	$ 229	$ 229	Tuition	$3,820
			Other	2,900
			Total	6,720
Parental contribution	1,571	1,571		
Tuition grant (only in certain states at present)	1,500	1,500		
Explicit self-help expectation	500[a]	850		
Residual to be met from other sources[b]	2,920 to 4,920	2,570		

10. Upper-income student attending low-cost community college as commuter. Family income = $35,000.

	Existing policies	Carnegie Council recommendations	Educational costs	
Basic Grant	0	0	Tuition	$ 200
			Other	2,400
			Total	2,600
Parental contribution	$2,600	$2,600		
Tuition grant	0	0		
Explicit self-help expectation[d]	0	0		
Residual to be met from other sources	0	0		

11. Upper-income student attending moderate-cost public four-year college as resident, lower-division. Family income = $35,000.

	Existing policies	Carnegie Council recommendations	Educational costs	
Basic Grant	0	0	Tuition	$ 650
			Other	2,500
			Total	3,150
Parental contribution	$3,150	$3,150		
Tuition grant	0	0		
Explicit self-help expectation[d]	0	0		
Residual to be met from other sources	0	0		

(continued on next page)

Table 2 *(continued)*

	Existing policies	Carnegie Council recommen- dations	Educational costs

12. Upper-income student attending high-cost private four-year college as resident, lower-division. Family income = $35,000.

Basic Grant	0	0	Tuition	$3,820
			Other	2,900
			Total	6,720
Parental contribution	$5,680	$5,680		
Tuition grant	0	0		
Explicit self-help expectation[d]	0	0		
Residual to be met from other sources[c]	1,040	1,040		

[a]Assumes CSS/ACT schedule is used in determining eligibility for state tuition grant; this schedule calls for about $500 in savings from summer earnings.

[b]Other sources may be College Work-Study award or SEOG grant (for needy students), borrowing, additional earnings, additional parental contribution, college grant, or miscellaneous.

[c]Assumes use of CSS/ACT schedule by student aid officer.

[d]There is no explicit self-help expectation, because the student is assumed not to be eligible for student aid from publicly financed sources; he or she might qualify for aid from college sources, and the college might require self-help.

Source: Carnegie Council. Parental contributions are derived from Table 4.

4. *Special provisions benefiting disadvantaged students who may have difficulty meeting the self-help expectation or face other unusual circumstances,* including (1) the 10 percent override in the Basic Grant program, (2) use of SEOG funds to meet such special needs, and (3) preference in College Work-Study awards.

5. *Greatly improved opportunity for all needy students to receive tuition grants,* under our recommendations for the SSIG program.

6. *Avoidance of an additional shift in funds in the form of student grants or tuition tax credits to upper-middle- and upper-income families.*

Figure 3. Comparison of sources of support for typical students under existing policies and Carnegie Council recommendations, 1982-83 (in 1979 dollars)

☐ Self-help expectation (in some cases only at present)   ▨ Parental contribution   ⊡ Tuition grant (Carnegie)

☐ Basic grant   ▨ Residual to be met from other sources

1. Lower-income student attending low-cost community college as commuter. Family income = $6,000. Tuition = $200; other educational costs = $2,400; total costs = $2,600.

$500 $850 $1,250

Existing policies

Carnegie Council

$800 $1,800

2. Lower-income student attending moderate-cost public four-year college as resident, lower division. Family income = $6,000. Tuition = $650; other educational costs = $2,500; total costs = $3,150.

$500 $1,575 $1,075

$850 $1,800 $400 $100

3. Lower-middle-income student attending low-cost community college as commuter. Family income = $15,000. Tuition = $200; other educational costs = $2,400; total costs = $2,600.

$500 $850 $717 $533

$800 $1,256 $544

4. Lower-middle-income student attending high-cost private four-year college as resident, lower division. Family income = $15,000. Tuition = $3,820; other educational costs = $2,900; total costs = $6,720.

$500 $1,083 $717 $4,420

$850 $1,256 $544 $1,500 $2,570

5. Upper-middle-income student attending moderate-cost public four-year college as resident, lower division. Family income = $23,000. Tuition = $650; other educational costs = $2,500; total costs = $3,150.

$500 $229 $1,571 $850

$850 $229 $1,571 $400 $100

6. Upper-middle-income student attending high-cost private four-year college as resident, lower division. Family income = $23,000. Tuition = $3,820; other educational costs = $2,900; total costs = $6,720.

$500 $229 $1,571 $4,420

$850 $229 $1,571 $1,500 $2,570

Source: Adapted from Table 2.

7. *Equitable access to loans for those lower-income students who find it necessary to borrow.*
8. *Simplification of rules and procedures.*
9. *A much higher degree of certainty about the total amount of aid for which a student would be eligible* (see Table 4).

Figure 3 and Table 2 provide illustrations of how typical students would be affected if the Council's recommendations were adopted. They show clearly the following results:

1. The lower-income student at the lower-division level would receive a Basic Grant of $1,800 in virtually all cases (except where the family has large assets), whereas at present his or her Basic Grant is reduced sharply by the 50-percent-of-cost limitation and by the ceiling of $1,500 on allowable subsistence costs if attending a lower-cost commuter college, and it is also reduced somewhat if attending a moderate-cost public four-year college. Only the lower-income student attending a comparatively high-cost college ($3,600 or more) receives the full Basic Grant.
2. Only in certain states does a student at present receive a tuition grant of the amount indicated in Table 2 (moreover, these amounts are illustrative of amounts available in certain state scholarship programs, but awards actually vary a good deal from state to state). Under Carnegie Council recommendations, the inducement to states to follow federal policies relating to scholarship programs would be far greater because of the greatly increased federal matching funds. Tuition grants would become much more certain and in many cases larger in amount, although in some cases (chiefly those of students attending low-cost public institutions) they would be reduced somewhat compared with present awards because of the $250 self-help expectation.
3. The explicit self-help expectation would apply uniformly, except that it would be larger for upper-division than for lower-division students. At present, a student may be expected to have about $500 to $700 in savings from summer employment (a smaller amount than we recommend) if he or

she receives aid under a program using the CSS/ACT parental contribution schedule—that is, one of the campus-based programs, some of the state scholarship programs, or the college's own aid program in some cases. Under our recommendations, the self-help expectation would become much more certain.

4. As a result of these changed policies, the residual amount that the student would have to meet from other sources would be greatly reduced and would become much more certain. In fact, the residual would be minimal except for those students attending relatively high-cost private colleges.

5. All students from families in the $6,000 to $18,000 income range would benefit from our recommended shift to the CSS/ACT parental contribution schedule.

Institutions. Table 3 shows how grant funds made available under our recommendations would be distributed among institutions. The net result would not significantly alter the existing distribution. Approximately 36 percent of the funds would aid students in private institutions, and 64 percent would benefit those in public institutions. Under existing policies, the overall proportion of funds flowing to students in private institutions is also 36 percent.

We make the following concluding notations:

• Some states are already considering raising tuition in public institutions of higher education in order to capture the maximum federal funds, as well as to reduce net costs to the state. Such actions will increase costs to the federal government (and may increase state scholarship costs also). We have no way of calculating the potential amounts involved.

• The basic problem for "middle-income" families is a disproportionate rise in taxes as compared with money income, particularly as they rise into higher income brackets, and not in costs of attending college. Offsetting the cost of attending college benefits only those families with children in college, not all families; and only 10 percent of families with children in college face the costs of attendance at higher-cost private

Table 3. Total grant funds by type of institution
(millions of 1979 dollars)

	Regular Basic Grants	Discretionary Basic Grants	Federal/state tuition grants	SEOG grants	Total	Percent
Public two-year[a]	1,243	124	57	11	1,435	26%
Public four-year						
Less than $700 tuition[b]	797	80	225	42	1,144	20
More than $700 tuition[c]	538	54	383	71	1,046	18
Private						
Less than $1,950 tuition[d]	244	24	365	68	701	12
$1,951 - $2,600 tuition[e]	164	16	298	55	533	9
More than $2,601 tuition[f]	251	25	506	94	876	15
Total	3,237	323	1,834	340	5,735	100%

[a] An estimated 930 institutions enrolling an estimated 2.3 million students more than half time.
[b] An estimated 310 institutions enrolling an estimated 2.1 million students more than half time.
[c] An estimated 250 institutions enrolling an estimated 1.7 million students more than half time.
[d] An estimated 540 institutions enrolling an estimated 700 thousand students more than half time.
[e] An estimated 280 institutions enrolling an estimated 500 thousand students more than half time.
[f] An estimated 820 institutions enrolling an estimated 900 thousand students more than half time.

Source: Carnegie Council staff estimates.

colleges. Thus, at best, "middle-income" assistance is a very partial solution to a more general problem.

- The only really great "deficit" in enrollment rates is for black males from the bottom quartile of the income range; partially offset by higher participation by this group in the armed services where they do acquire skills. This is the segment of the population where greater equality of opportunity through college attendance is least realized. It also experiences the highest rate of unemployment. The programs we propose would make attendance in college by members of this group more feasible financially, but they by no means would guarantee greater participation.

- We urge strongly that our proposals be viewed as interrelated. It would not be wise to pick up one item at a time without consideration of the impact on other items. The "trade-offs" of reductions and increases are carefully balanced; and neither reductions nor increases should be considered all by themselves.

There is no final solution to all student aid problems. Changes will need to be made as experience accumulates and/or conditions change. However, we are now coming close to realization of an adequate and equitable program for the conditions of the current period.

2

Specific
Recommendations

A Self-Help Requirement

One of the most pressing needs in student aid policies is to clarify and specify the role of student self-help.

Holding a part-time job is an important source of financing a college education. Yet earnings play an uncertain and ambiguous role in student aid. Some colleges require students who apply for aid to meet part of their educational expenses through earnings; others do not. Under Basic Grant policies, expected or actual earnings are not deducted from a student's grant, whereas under the CSS/ACT schedule there is an expectation of summer earnings.

Borrowing plays a similarly ambiguous role. Some colleges require that a portion of a student's aid package take the form of a loan, but this is by no means a uniform practice.

We believe that the time has come to assume that, under normal circumstances, a student applying for aid should be expected to contribute substantially to his or her college expenses. Students might substitute borrowing for all or a portion of expected earnings, especially in situations in which jobs are hard to find, but we believe that most students will prefer summer employment and part-time jobs during termtime to indebtedness.

There are many reasons for advocating a self-help expectation:

1. It will help meet the problems posed by the growing proportion of students declaring themselves independent of their parents and will facilitate devising equitable policies for providing assistance to needy part-time and adult students.
2. There is a case for student self-help in view of the economic benefits the student can normally expect from a college education.
3. An earnings expectation is consistent with the changing status of young people in our society. They have been granted legal majority, and they tend to achieve adult status in terms of social behavior earlier than college-age young people did in the past.
4. With the extension of student grants to young people from middle-income families, the relative contribution of the taxpayer, compared with that of students and parents, has been increased. An earnings expectation for all students applying for aid would help to redress the balance.

On the basis of the data available on student earnings, we believe that it is reasonable to expect lower-division students to contribute about $600 to annual college expenses ($850 if they also participate in the SSIG program). Upper-division students, having successfully completed two years of college, should be capable of working somewhat more without interfering with educational achievement—we believe about $1,000 is a reasonably normal expectation for these students ($1,250 if they also participate in the SSIG program). It is true that women earn less than men—this is the case for women students as well as for women in the labor force generally—but our data show that the earnings requirements we propose fall below the average earnings of women who are employed both during the college year and in the summer. Clearly men would be able to meet the earnings requirement more easily than women, but we believe this inequity is preferable to a cumbersome and controversial policy that would call for smaller earnings expectations for women than for men. The self-help expectations should be adjusted upward by Congress from time to time.

Our data also show that students from the lowest parental income quartile are less likely to be employed than students from families with more income. The difference is particularly pronounced in the case of summer employment. This may reflect the fact that summer jobs are harder to get in the inner city and rural areas where many lower-income students live or that summer earnings must be contributed to families for subsistence. In some cases, such students may expect to qualify for student aid and therefore feel less need for summer earnings. The tendency for fewer lower-income students to be employed helps to explain the lower percentages employed among blacks and other minority groups, a large proportion of whom are from lower-income families. On the other hand, blacks who are employed during the college year tend to earn more than employed white students, suggesting longer hours of work.

For a variety of reasons, some students—especially those from lower-income families—are likely to have greater difficulty in meeting an earnings requirement than others. We therefore propose that a portion of Basic Grant funds be set aside to meet the needs of such students, that preference be granted lower-income students and women in awarding CWS grants where the number of applicants exceeds the number of CWS jobs available, and that students be expected to opt for borrowing rather than contributing earnings in appropriate cases.

We also propose that the greater part of the normal self-help expectation be allocated to noninstructional costs through the Basic Grant program and the remainder to tuition through the SSIG program.

Recommendation 1: *Students should normally be expected to contribute significantly from their own earnings toward college expenses, as a condition of eligibility for student aid. An earnings expectation should gradually be imposed in the Basic Grant program and by 1982-83 should amount to $600 for lower-division students and to $1,000 for upper-division students, and a modest additional contribution of $250 should be required in the SSIG program. A student should be permitted to meet the self-help expectation wholly or partially through borrowing as an alternative form of self-help.*

Expanding the Role of the College Work-Study Program

Under policies embodying a self-help requirement, the CWS program should play an even more important role than it does now. A recent study has shown that participation in federal work-study programs tends to enhance student persistence, especially among women and blacks. Somewhat surprisingly, also, whether the job is academic or nonacademic does not seem to make an appreciable difference in this result, although the job should be limited to not more than 20 hours a week (Wenc, 1977; and Astin, 1975). Participation in a work-study program or other on-campus employment appears to increase a student's sense of identification with his or her college.

Employment opportunities are relatively unfavorable for students in small-town colleges and for minority students in inner-city areas. They are also sometimes less favorable for women than for men. Thus, we believe that preference should be given to students who cannot find employment in the private economy when CWS funds are inadequate to meet the needs of all applicants.

Recent moves by the Congress and the administration to increase the appropriation for the College Work-Study program are to be commended. The funds allocated to the program have been increased from $300 million in 1974-75 to $550 million in the 1978-79 budget (to be expended in 1979-80). We believe, however, that additional substantial increases should be approved. Appropriations for the program should gradually be increased to $900 million by 1972-83 from the current $550 million.

We also believe that there is a strong case for gradual elimination of the family income eligibility conditions in the CWS program. Such a policy, in our view, would be greatly preferable to any additional extension of grant aid to students from upper-middle- or upper-income families or to tuition tax credits as a way of helping the families of such students. It would also be consistent with the desirability of eliminating social distinctions between students from low-income and high-income families.

Recommendation 2: *The annual appropriation for the College Work-Study (CWS) program should gradually be increased to $900 million (in constant 1979 dollars) by 1982-83. Family income eligibility conditions should gradually be removed from the program, but preference in awarding employment opportunities under the program should be given to students, especially women and minorities, who have difficulty in finding jobs in the private employment market.*

Meeting the Problems of the Independent Student

A self-help requirement would also make a substantial contribution to resolving the difficult policy problems posed by the growth of the proportion of student aid applicants seeking independent status. Much of the concern about this trend arises over the possibility that, when their children are granted independent status, parents who could afford to contribute to their children's educational expenses are being relieved of their financial responsibilities. In fact, available data do not suggest that this type of abuse of student aid is widespread, for independent students are more likely to be from lower-income families than are dependent students; but the possibility of such abuse does exist, and it is quite possible that increasing advantage will be taken of it.

In particular, we believe that the probability of abuse may increase as a result of one of the changes brought about by the Middle-Income Student Assistance Act of 1978, under which the "family size offset" for an independent student without dependents was raised from $1,100 to $3,400.[1] This means that $3,400 of such a student's income would be disregarded in determining eligibility for a Basic Grant and that almost every independent student without dependents could qualify for the maximum Basic Grant. Under these conditions, the temptation to seek independent status in order to avoid a parental contribution would be very great. We believe that it would have been wiser for Congress to increase the family size offset more gradu-

[1]Congress did not appropriate the funds needed to finance this provision in adopting the 1978-79 budget, nor did the administration include them in the 1979-80 budget.

ally, if at all, in order to evaluate the results. The policy needs to be reconsidered. It is undoubtedly a desirable provision for some groups of independent students, such as divorced or separated women, but its invitation to abuse on the part of students who would otherwise be assisted by their parents is a serious problem.

Our proposal for a self-help expectation would help to prevent abuse on the part of students seeking a "free ride."

We believe, also, that more objective criteria should be developed for determining independent status. Existing rules are difficult to enforce and at the same time intrusive in their concern with intrafamily relationships. New general rules should be developed that would take into account the applicant's age, whether he or she has dependents, whether he or she is an orphan, and the number of years during which he or she has essentially been self-supporting. The more difficult cases of young students who do not meet such criteria could then be handled on a case-by-case basis by student aid officers, who would have access to detailed family financial information.

We also propose certain changes in policies relating to independent students with dependents. In general, the family contribution schedule for such families should be the same as for parents of dependent students (independent students with dependents are expected to make a higher contribution at present). Student aid should be available, however, only for the member of the family who is enrolled and not for dependents.[2] However, exceptions to this rule could be made, and reductions in the self-help expectation should be permitted in appropriate cases, such as those in which a mother enrolled as a student requires child care services.

Recommendation 3: *The self-help expectation should normally be applicable to independent as well as to dependent students, and the recently pronounced legislative increase in the "family*

---

[2] Aid for dependents of independent students is currently permissable under the SEOG program and other "campus-based" programs, but available funds do not often permit student aid officers to provide such aid.

size offset" for independent students without dependents should be reconsidered by Congress. More objective criteria for determining independent status should be developed—criteria that would take into account the applicant's age, whether he or she has dependents, whether he or she is an orphan, and the number of years during which he or she has been self-supporting. The more difficult cases of applicants who do not meet such criteria should be handled by student aid officers. Independent students with dependents should be subject to the same parental contribution schedule as parents of dependent students (with adjustments to meet unusual circumstances), and should not ordinarily receive student aid for their dependents.

Equitable Provision for Noninstructional Costs

We believe that equitable provision for noninstructional costs should be the first responsibility of a need-based student aid program. Noninstructional costs include basic subsistence expenses and the costs of such essential items as books, supplies, and necessary transportation expenses. Meeting these costs is far more difficult for students from lower-income and disadvantaged families than it is for young people from more affluent families. In a lower-income family, the earnings of a college-age son or daughter may be sorely needed to contribute to family subsistence needs, especially where income is inadequate because of the disability, unemployment, or death of the household head. In more technical terms, foregone earnings are a more serious sacrifice for students from disadvantaged families than for those from middle- and upper-income families.

Partly for this reason, we recommend that the Basic Grant program should be designed to cover noninstructional costs of needy students. Moreover, noninstructional costs vary much less from college to college and from one part of the country to another than do tuition and required fees. Thus they lend themselves to provision by the basic federal student aid program, whereas provision for tuition is more appropriately a responsibility of the federal-state SSIG program. That is so because tuition in public higher education—and thus the tuition gap between public and private institutions in a given state—is determined at the state level.

Recommendation 4: *Student assistance under the Basic Grant program should be designed to cover noninstructional costs of needy students.*

Reconciling Subsistence Needs and Self-Help Expectations

If the Basic Grant program is to provide adequately for subsistence needs and other noninstructional costs of needy students and incorporate a self-help expectation, the size of the maximum grant should be increased gradually over the years from 1979-80 to 1982-83. We commend Congress and the administration for supporting increases in the appropriations for the program in the last few years, which have made it a true entitlement program, and for raising the maximum grant to $1,800. However, noninstructional costs have been rising and additional increases can be expected in the future. For 1978-79, noninstructional costs for student commuters at various types of institutions have been estimated to be in the neighborhood of $2,000 (Suchar, Ivens, and Jacobson, 1978, p. vii). They are considerably higher—around $2,700—for students living away from home, because charges for board and room are higher than estimated board and room costs of student commuters (Suchar, Ivens, and Jacobson, 1978). We believe that the maximum Basic Grant award should be increased gradually over a period of three years to $2,400 to cover noninstructional costs adequately for the average student. In practice, this would mean that the maximum grant would normally be $1,800 for lower-division students and $1,400 for upper-division students, taking the self-help expectation into account. Since under present policies the maximum allowance for noninstructional costs for commuters is $1,500, the effect of our proposals would be to increase the maximum allowance for noninstructional costs for many lower-division students as well as for all students who would not be able to meet the self-help expectation because of special circumstances.

Future adjustments in the Basic Grant ceiling to meet rising costs will be needed from time to time, but should be left to Congressional determination.

Recommendation 5: *The maximum award in the Basic Grant* *program should be increased gradually to $2,400 by 1982-83. This would mean that the maximum grant in practice would normally be $1,800 for lower-division and $1,400 for upper-division students, after taking account of the self-help expectation.*

Providing for Exceptional Cases

Although we believe that a self-help expectation is a reasonable requirement of a student aid program, some students will have unusual difficulty in meeting such a requirement because they attend college in areas where part-time jobs are particularly hard to find, or they are physically handicapped, or they need to take extra courses beyond the normal load because of poor preparation for college work, or they are too young (age 16-17) to have good job opportunities. We therefore propose that Congress appropriate an additional sum for the Basic Grant program, amounting to 10 percent of estimated costs for the usual types of grants under the program, to meet the needs of these students in unusual circumstances or for whom the earnings expectation would create difficulties.

Some of these students would be members of minority groups living in inner-city areas, where unemployment rates are exceptionally high. Others would be students in colleges located in small communities where few suitable jobs are available. Others would be disabled, while still others would be carrying a heavy course load because of the need for orientation to college-level education, or they would be less than 18 years of age. Such students could receive up to $2,400 a year by 1982-83.

Availability of such discretionary funds would facilitate uniform treatment under simplified rules for the more usual student applicant. It would also facilitate accommodation of the genuinely needy independent student without opening the door to abuse by students seeking independent status for the purpose of relieving their parents of expected contributions.

Recommendation 6: *Congress should allocate, over and above the sum needed to meet normal expected costs of the Basic Grant program, an additional 10 percent for discretionary use in the administration of the program at the campus level, including* *waiver or modification of the self-help expectation for students whose employment opportunities are impaired by residence in inner city or rural areas, disabilities, the need for a heavy course load, exceptional family circumstances, or college entrance at an unusually early age.*

Removing the 50-Percent-of-Cost Limitation

With adoption of our proposal for a self-help expectation under the Basic Grant program, one important reason for the existing limitation of a student's grant to no more than 50 percent of the student's total educational costs is removed. Part of the rationale for the 50-percent-of-cost limitation has been that students attending low-cost commuter institutions should not have their full costs of attendance subsidized by the general public. In fact, under our proposal a lower-division student attending an institution with costs of $2,500 or more (and there are very few institutions with costs lower than that) would receive a grant amounting to 72 percent or less of total costs (the higher the costs, the smaller the percentage), while an upper-division student would receive 56 percent or less. These percentages would not apply to the exceptional cases discussed above.

The 50-percent-of-cost limitation has tended to discriminate against low-income students whose most feasible option is attendance at a low-cost commuter institution, and yet its retention has been vigorously supported by some representatives of private institutions, for fear that low-income students would be even more likely to attend low-cost public institutions if their full costs could be covered by a Basic Grant. However, the impact of our Basic Grant recommendations should be considered in conjunction with our recommendations for expansion of the SSIG program. If our recommendations relating to SSIG are adopted, not only will the competitive position of private institutions in states now lacking adequate state scholarship programs be greatly improved but so will the capacity of lower-income students to attend private institutions.

Recommendation 7: *The present limitation of a Basic Grant to 50 percent of a student's total educational costs should be re-*

moved, since our recommendations for a self-help expectation in the Basic Grant program, together with our recommendations for substantial expansion of the SSIG program, remove the rationale for retention of the limitation.

Preventing Erosion of Need-Based Student Aid

With the adoption of the Middle-Income Student Assistance Act of 1978, a major step has been taken to extend student grants to the children of upper-middle-income families. We believe that this movement need go no farther, and, in particular, we oppose adoption of tuition tax credits for the families of college students.

The evidence that young people from middle-income families have been discouraged from college attendance by rising costs is unconvincing. Only among young white males has there been a drop in attendance rates, affecting all income groups, and this decline is probably chiefly attributable to the removal of the draft. In addition, incomes of average upper-middle-income families have more than kept pace with rising costs of college attendance, when allowance is made for the fact that expected parental contributions have risen much less than income (Figure 2). And, as Figure 4 shows, middle- and upper-middle-income families have experienced more pronounced increases in income than either lower- or upper-income families, whose income increases have barely kept pace with the cost of living.

We believe that Congress was wise in choosing to help upper-middle-income families by liberalizing student aid, rather than by adopting tuition tax credits, because their approach preserves the principle of need-based student aid, whereas tuition tax credits do not. We also oppose tuition tax credits for the following reasons:

1. They would be very costly to the U.S. Treasury, while at the same time providing such nominal relief to individual families that the pressure to increase the amounts of the credits, once adopted, would inevitably be very strong.
2. The temptation for colleges and universities to raise their tuition by the amount of the tax credit would be very great,

Figure 4. Relative changes in income for families at different income levels, in current and constant dollars, 1967 to 1978

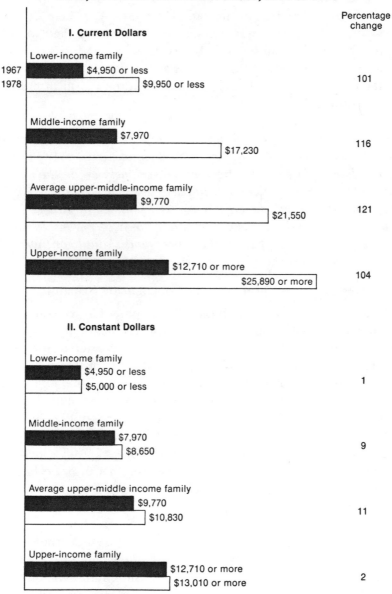

Sources: Computed from data in U.S. Bureau of the Census (1969, Table 9, and 1978, Table 6); and President of the United States (1978, p. 313). Data on family income for 1978 projected on the basis of trends from 1972 to 1977.

thereby nullifying the relief and rendering the aid to families self-defeating.

3. Tuition tax credits are not an effective way of helping private institutions compete for students, because they would not reduce the tuition gap between public and private colleges, and the bulk of the benefits (if any) would go to the far more numerous families whose children enroll in public institutions.

Recommendation 8: *The movement to provide aid to students from "middle-income" families should go no further. Any additional changes in this direction would seriously erode the need-based character of student aid. In particular, we strongly oppose adoption of tuition tax credits for the families of college students as a regressive and self-defeating form of parental relief. The central purpose of student aid programs should continue to be the encouragement of equality of opportunity.*

Need for a Uniform Parental Contribution Schedule

The liberalization of the Basic Grant parental contribution schedule that was adopted under the provisions of the Middle-Income Student Assistance Act of 1978 has created a situation in which the need for a uniform parental contribution schedule is imperative. As Figure 5 and Table 4 show, the expected parental contribution under the Basic Grant schedule is higher than the contribution expected under the CSS/ACT schedule for families with incomes up to $18,000. For higher family incomes, however, the contribution under the CSS/ACT schedule not only is larger but increases more sharply because it calls for progressively higher proportional contributions from families as income rises, whereas the Basic Grant schedule calls for a flat contribution rate of 10.5 percent.

The situation has become very unstable because there will be pressure from parents, students, and student aid officers to shift from the CSS/ACT to the new Basic Grant schedule in connection with federal campus-based student aid and state scholarship programs, at least as the schedule relates to higher incomes. The new Basic Grant schedule is, in fact, inoperative in

Figure 5. Average expected parental contributions for dependent students, by family income: Comparison of CSS/ACT and revised Basic Grant schedule for 1979-80

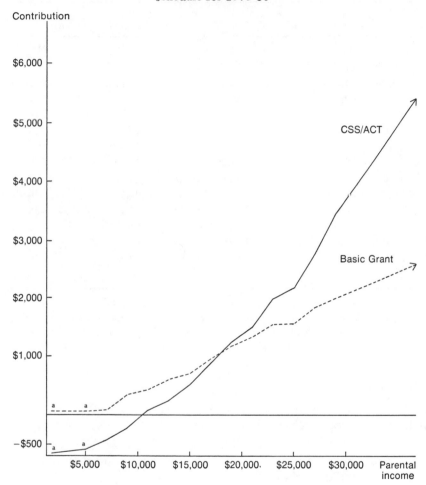

[a]Parental contributions are expected of these low-income families where assets are large, as in some farm families.

Source: Table 4.

relation to the Basic Grant program itself for families with incomes above $25,000 because at that point the expected parental contribution rises to $1,600 or more, and thus, with a maximum grant of $1,800 and a minimum grant of $200, the

Table 4. Comparison of Basic Grant and CSS/ACT: Average expected
parental contributions for dependent students, 1979-80

Total income	CSS/ACT	Basic Grant	Percent difference
$ 0 - 4,000	$-670	$ 81	NA
4,000 - 6,000	-600	51	NA
6,000 - 8,000	-439	111	NA
8,000 · 10,000	-220	355	NA
10,000 - 12,000	57	437	666
12,000 - 14,000	245	610	148
14,000 - 16,000	544	717	31
16,000 - 18,000	902	983	8
18,000 - 20,000	1,256	1,217	-3
20,000 - 22,000	1,520	1,361	-10
22,000 - 24,000	2,113	1,571	-25
24,000 - 26,000	2,215	1,593	-28
26,000 - 28,000	2,839	1,883	-33
28,000 - 30,000	3,380	2,016	-40
30,000+	6,341	3,052	-51

Source: Data provided by the College Scholarship Service (CSS) of the College Entrance Examination Board. Simulations based on 2,000 random cases of dependent
student CSS filers. These are preliminary estimates. Further simulations (including
estimates varied by family size, number of dependents in college, asset levels) are
being conducted on a sample of 10,000 cases.

student becomes ineligible for assistance. However, such a student could readily receive more generous aid under campus-
based or state scholarship programs if the new Basic Grant
schedule became the standard, while Basic Grant recipients
could receive a more generous total package of aid if they qualified under these other programs.

We believe that such a trend would be a major mistake, for
the new schedule is so liberal in the upper-income ranges that its
widespread use would virtually do away with the concept of
need in federally supported student grant programs.

We advocate instead adoption of the CSS/ACT schedule as
the standard for all federally supported student aid programs,
except for such minor adjustments of contributions for families
in the $22,000 to $25,000 income range as would preserve eligi-

bility for a small Basic Grant for their children. (At present, the expected parental contribution for families in this income range under the CSS/ACT schedule is about $2,000, thus ruling out eligibility for a Basic Grant with a ceiling of $1,800.) The CSS/ACT schedule was liberalized markedly between 1974 and 1975, greatly reducing expected parental contributions and resulting in a situation in which even students from families in the $30,000 to $35,000 income range could expect some grant aid.

Applying the more generous new Basic Grant schedule to these upper-income ranges would be altogether unjustified, while shifting to the CSS/ACT schedule for the Basic Grant program would result in more adequate aid for students from families in the income range from $6,000 to $18,000. In Figure 6, we show how our recommendations for the Basic Grant program would work out if the CSS/ACT schedule were adopted (except for the $22,000 to $25,000 family income range, where the new Basic Grant schedule would apply) and if our self-help expectations were adopted. Implicit in our self-help expectations is the elimination of Basic Grants for upper-division students from families with incomes of $18,000 or more, except for those students in unusual circumstances who would qualify for assistance from the 10 percent Basic Grant override.

The CSS/ACT schedule should apply not only to Basic Grants and to the federal SEOG program but also to federal matching of state funds under the SSIG program. The impact of this policy on state programs will be discussed more fully below.

If the CSS/ACT schedule does become the standard for these programs, however, it is imperative that a number of complexities (such as graduated allowances for accumulating savings for retirement) be removed from the schedule and that the application form be greatly simplified. This is in line with our general proposal for simplification of regulations and procedures.

Recommendation 9: *A simplified CSS/ACT parental contribution schedule should be adopted by the federal government to apply to federal student grant programs and to federal matching of state funds under the State Student Incentive Grant program,*

Figure 6. Basic Grants for which students would be eligible, using
CSS/ACT or Basic Grant family contribution schedule, assuming a
maximum grant of $2,400 and self-help expectations recommended by
the Carnegie Council

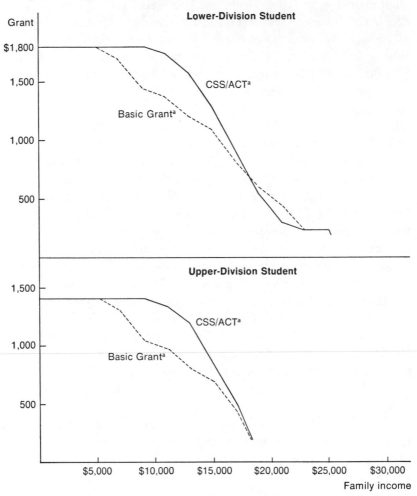

[a]Assumes the expected parental contribution for a four-member family with one
child in college and no unusual circumstances; also assumes that CSS/ACT schedule is
adjusted to correspond to the Basic Grant schedule for families in the $22,000 to
$25,000 income range.

Source: Carnegie Council (derived from data in Table 4).

after minor adjustments to preserve eligibility for Basic Grants for students from families in the $22,000 to $25,000 income range.

Limiting the Duration of Student Aid

The Basic Grant program, as well as other student aid programs, can be abused by students with irregular patterns of participation in higher education, who may stop out for a time without having completed a degree program and later return. We believe that eligibility for Basic Grants should be limited to a total of two years at a two-year college and to four years at a four-year college (on a full-time equivalent basis) and that students who are not making normal progress toward a degree should lose their eligibility for student aid.

Recommendation 10: *Eligibility for Basic Grants and other types of federally assisted student aid should be limited to two years at a two-year college and four years at a four-year college (on a full-time equivalent basis) and to students making normal progress toward a degree.*[3]

The SSIG Program

We believe that the federal-state State Student Incentive Grant (SSIG) program should be the primary means of providing tuition assistance for needy students. To this end, we recommend a large increase in federal appropriations for the program, in line with our earlier recommendations (Carnegie Council, 1975, 1977). There are several important reasons why tuition assistance can best be provided by a federal-state program.

1. Tuition policy in public higher education is determined at the state level, and thus it is at that level that the size of the tuition gap between private and public institutions of higher

---

[3]The period could be lengthened to five years for certain degree programs, as in engineering, that normally require five years for a bachelor's degree, as under existing policies.

education is also determined. Just as there is a case for designing the Basic Grant program to meet noninstructional costs, which vary little from state to state, there is a corresponding need to structure the SSIG program to aid needy students in meeting tuition costs. In fact, many of the state scholarship programs do limit state grants to covering a portion of tuition and fee expenses.

2. Adequate federal matching grants will provide a powerful incentive for increases in state appropriations for scholarship programs in the many states in which such appropriations are seriously inadequate. Although the SSIG program has demonstrated its effectiveness in inducing states to adopt programs of student aid where they were previously nonexistent, it has been much less effective—chiefly because of small federal appropriations—in inducing such states to provide funds large enough to provide for needy students. All of the states with the largest scholarship programs had developed their programs before the federal SSIG program was adopted under the 1972 amendments.

3. In the absence of special federal assistance, state scholarship programs are likely to discourage interstate movement of students and thus are likely to lead to excessive provincialism in higher education. In fact, according to the most recent survey of the National Association of State Scholarship and Grant Programs (1978, p. 24), state grants are now portable (available for all students enrolling outside their state of residence) only in Connecticut, Delaware, Massachusetts, Rhode Island, and Vermont (along with the District of Columbia and the Virgin Islands). Several states, including New Jersey and Pennsylvania, which formerly provided for portability in some or all of their scholarship programs, have recently taken steps to limit portability to states that reciprocate (Hansen, 1979).

4. As matters stand, there is enormous variation among the states in their willingness to finance state scholarship programs. Just five states—California, Illinois, New York, Pennsylvania, and New Jersey—account for 65.7 percent of appropriations for 1978-79. At the other extreme are states

with extremely small expenditures. We believe that a decisive increase in federal matching funds would induce the lagging states to allocate enough money to provide for needy students.

In this connection, it is important to point out that our recommendations are aimed at equalizing the burden of states in providing scholarships for needy students, as well as inducing larger appropriations from lagging states. We do not believe that an equitable federal-state student aid system will be achieved until this is accomplished. States with exceptionally large state scholarship financing burdens would be able to reduce their own appropriations if much larger federal matching funds were available. In 1978-79, federal matching funds amounted to only 2 percent of New York's expenditures on need-based undergraduate state scholarships. They were also an extremely small percentage of total scholarship funds in other states that had had large programs before SSIG was adopted. On the other hand, federal matching funds amounted to 50 percent of the total (but very small) appropriations in many of the states that had been induced to adopt state programs under the impetus of SSIG.

In this respect, our proposed policies differ markedly from those espoused by some members of Congress who have advocated moving the base date for federal matching forward. Under existing policies, the federal government matches increases in state funds since 1971-72 (for states that had state student aid programs then) or since the "second fiscal year preceding the fiscal year in which the state initially received funds" (for states with new programs). Members of Congress who would move the matching date forward to some year much more recent than 1971-72 are interested primarily in inducing increases in state appropriations, regardless of the impact on equitable distribution of matching funds among the states.

In addition to proposing a major increase in federal expenditures for the SSIG program, we recommend the following changes in federal provisions for the program:

1. Federal matching funds, which now cover one half of state grants up to a maximum of $1,500, should be modified to cover one half of state grants (for tuition and required fees only) up to a maximum of $1,500 over and above the first $250 of tuition, which should normally be met from the student's earnings or other forms of self-help.

2. In order to induce states to make tuition grants portable, we recommend that the federal government pay 75 percent of the cost of those tuition grants that are used by a student to enroll in a state other than his or her state of residence. In other words, the federal government would match on a three-to-one, rather than the usual one-to-one, basis in the case of grants used outside of the student's state of residence. We believe that this overmatching would provide a powerful inducement to states to make their grants portable, although some states might wish to limit portability to states that reciprocate.

3. We recommend moving the matching date back to 1969-70 for those states that had eligible state scholarship programs at that time.

4. We also recommend that the CSS/ACT parental contribution schedule should apply to federal matching in the SSIG program.[4] There are a number of states in which a relatively large proportion of the recipients of state aid are in upper-middle-income families. States would be free, under our proposal, to use parental contribution schedules that were more liberal than the CSS/ACT schedule, but they would not receive federal matching funds for amounts of student aid that would not be available under that schedule.

In this connection, states would also be free to follow more generous policies than those we recommend in other respects, but they would be eligible for federal matching funds only for those amounts of student aid indicated by the policies

---

[4]Under the Education Amendments of 1972, the Commissioner of Education has the power to approve criteria of need established by states, but in practice the states have largely been free to apply their own criteria.

we propose. California, for example, now makes grants up to a maximum of $2,900 and probably would not wish to lower this ceiling,[5] but it would be eligible for federal matching up to only $1,500 (and after allowing for the $250 self-help expectation).

Another important point is that, even if a uniform parental contribution schedule is in effect for both federal student aid and a state scholarship program, state aid will inevitably be available for students from upper-middle-income families and from some upper-income families under the coordinated federal-state policies that we propose. This is because a large proportion of parents will meet all or most of their expected contribution in connection with noninstructional costs and will not be expected to make a contribution of appreciable size in connection with the state scholarship program. This effect is particularly important for families with incomes in the range of $20,000 to $35,000 (the effect varying, of course, with the cost of the college the student is attending).

We estimate the cost of the federal-state SSIG program under these proposed changes at $1,834 million (in constant 1979 dollars) by 1982-83, of which $917 million would represent federal expenditures and $917 million state expenditures. The 50-50 division between federal and state expenditures is somewhat accidental. Although the federal government would not match the approximately $200 million being spent by states in 1969-70, its additional costs for meeting 75 percent of portable grants are estimated at about $200 million, so that adjustments for these two items result in making federal costs equal to state costs.

Thus, our recommendations would call for an increase in the federal appropriation for SSIG from $77 million in 1979-80 to $917 million in 1982-83. This is a large increase, but, as Figure 1 and Table 1 show, the increase (plus our proposed increase in Basic Grant and in College Work-Study expenditures) would be offset by reductions in costs of other federal student

[5]The statutory ceiling is actually somewhat higher, but, according to the California Student Aid Commission, the working maximum is likely to be $2,900 in 1979-80 because of limitation of available funds.

aid programs so that overall expenditures on all student aid programs would decrease somewhat by 1982-83.

Our proposals would call for a net increase of about $152 million in state expenditures on scholarship programs, as compared with expenditures in 1978-79. However, this net increase would represent the difference between an increase of about $367 million for those states (the vast majority) that would have to increase their appropriations to qualify for full federal matching and a reduction of about $215 million for six states—California, Illinois, Minnesota, New Jersey, New York, and Wisconsin—that could reduce their expenditures, because they would receive far more federal funds than they do now.[6]

Another point that should be emphasized is that our recommendations relating to the maximum tuition grant imply that many students, especially those seeking to attend relatively high-cost institutions, will have to borrow to meet their full tuition costs unless they can earn more than the normal earnings expectation, receive aid from the college's own funds or from their parents, or succeed in finding the money in some other way. We do not regard this as an undesirable consequence of our proposal for structuring SSIG tuition grants, especially in view of the fact that institutions with high tuition do tend to have more student aid funds of their own, and a public policy designed to provide tuition grants that would match tuition costs at such institutions would be highly questionable.

Recommendation 11: *Total appropriations for the federal share of the SSIG program should be increased to $917 million by 1982-83, so that total federal-state funds for need-based undergraduate state scholarship programs would be large enough to provide tuition assistance to all needy undergraduates.*

Federal provisions should also be amended to (1) provide matching funds for grants to meet tuition expenses in excess of $250 up to a maximum of $1,500—the $250 being a self-help expectation for the student—or a total tuition of $1,750; (2)

---

[6]The reduction would be very small for California and would not apply if the state retained its policy of allowing a relatively high maximum grant.

increase the federal matching formula to 75 percent of the cost of grants awarded to students attending institutions in other states (limited to states that reciprocate, if the state prefers); (3) provide for matching increases in state appropriations from 1969-70 on; and (4) limit federal matching to amounts of student aid indicated when the CSS/ACT parental contribution schedule is used.

The SEOG Program

Although Congress specified under the Education Amendments of 1972 that Supplemental Educational Opportunity Grants (SEOG) should be awarded to students "of exceptional financial need," it is not clear that the program has conformed to that purpose.

We believe that, with a uniform self-help expectation and a greatly expanded SSIG program, the SEOG program can serve a more clear-cut purpose in providing student aid officers with funds that can be allocated to students who have exceptional need for grant assistance, either because of unusual family circumstances, or because of special difficulties in meeting the self-help requirement. Its role would be analogous to that of the special 10 percent augmentation of Basic Grant funds, but whereas these Basic Grant funds would be allocated for meeting noninstructional costs, SEOG funds would cover unusual needs for meeting tuition costs.

Recommendation 12: The Supplemental Educational Opportunity Grant (SEOG) program should be continued at approximately its 1979-80 level of funding, but assistance under the program should be designed for students who have difficulty in meeting tuition costs because of unusual family circumstances, difficulty in meeting the self-help requirement, or other special problems.

An Equitable and Accessible Loan Program

In the eyes of the general public, the chief problem with existing student loan programs has been a high rate of default. Recently the Office of Education has intensified its efforts to reduce defaults, with some apparent success. The latest reported overall default rate of about 11 percent in the Guaranteed Student Loan (GSL) program is somewhat lower than that reported earlier ("GSL Needs Sallie Mae's Help . . . ," 1978). The 19 percent default rate in the National Direct Student Loan (NDSL) program will be more difficult to reduce. In the view of some observers, however, there is no case for far-reaching changes in existing student loan programs if the default problem can be brought under control.

We do not agree. We find many serious inequities and deficiencies in existing student loan programs that can be corrected only by replacing them with a more unified and carefully structured program.

Although the Carnegie Council does not believe that loans should ever become the major source of student financing, especially for undergraduates, we do believe that an equitable and accessible loan program should be available as a supplement to other forms of student assistance, especially for upper-division students, and as an indispensable source of support for graduate and professional students.

Our 1975 recommendation for a National Student Loan Bank (which was modeled after a recommendation made by the Carnegie Commission in 1970) appeared to attract little attention in Congress, but there are indications, especially in the form of recent proposals for similar, though not identical, restructuring of loan programs, that higher priority will be placed on serious consideration of such proposals in the debates over the 1979 amendments.

Briefly, we identify the following weaknesses in the GSL program:

1. A basic problem of inequality of opportunity because of the inevitable preference of lenders for students from families with good credit standing.
2. The difficulty of ensuring student access to loans in a tight money market, especially when there is a lag in adjusting the "special allowance" that supplements the interest yield of GSL loans.
3. The lack of incentive for banks and other lenders to pursue

adequate collection procedures when loans are guaranteed
by the federal government.

4. A fundamental question as to whether interest subsidies, as
   opposed to deferral of interest until after graduation, are appropriate, especially now that they are available for students
   from all families, regardless of income.

5. The disadvantage of a short period of repayment—difficult
   to avoid when banks predominate among lenders—in view of
   the fact that incomes of college graduates are likely to be
   lower in the first ten years after graduation than they are
   later in life. Such a repayment period is particularly disad-
   vantageous for married women who leave the labor force to
   have children.

The NDSL program, through which funds have been made
available to colleges and universities since 1958, is also by no
means free of problems:

1. The 3 percent interest rate on NDSL loans, which was in line
   with prevailing rates when the program was established, has
   increasingly become an anachronism, involving serious inequities between the students who repay at this low rate and
   those who must pay the GSL rate of 7 percent.

2. Other inequities arise from the fact that colleges and universities have complete control over which students receive
   NDSL loans but much less control over GSL loans. There is
   an understandable tendency to give preference to able students in the allocation of NDSL funds.

3. The default rate in the NDSL program (about 19 percent) is
   even higher than in the GSL program.

We believe that these inequities, as well as excessive government subsidization, could be overcome by phasing out existing loan programs and replacing them with a National Student
Loan Bank (NSLB), including the following provisions:

1. The federal government should charter a National Student
   Loan Bank, a nonprofit private corporation to be financed
   by the sale of governmentally guaranteed securities. The

bank would be self-sustaining, except for administrative costs and the costs of loan cancellation owing to death or unusual circumstances.

2. The bank would make loans in amounts not to exceed a reasonable total per year, which would in no case exceed a student's cost of education minus any grant aid and minus the relevant earnings expectation for those students opting to meet the self-help expectation through earnings. To make certain that these limits were observed, the college's financial aid officer would be required by the bank to certify the application. No student would be permitted to borrow more than $500 in the first semester of his or her freshmen year. We propose this limit not only because we think an appropriate combination of student grants, parental contributions, and student earnings should prevent any need for substantial borrowing by beginning students but also because such a limit would severely discourage an important type of abuse of student loans by certain unscrupulous institutions of higher education that entice students to enroll with the aid of loans and by some student borrowers who are not serious about higher education.

3. Borrowers would be required to repay loans by paying approximately 1 percent of income each year for each $1,000 borrowed until the total loan and accrued interest was repaid (the exact amount to depend on projected rates of inflation). This level of repayment would permit the average income earner to repay his loan in about 20 years. (Lower earners would require a longer period.) Borrowers filing a joint tax return could elect an appropriately lower rate of repayment that would be applied to the combined income of the husband and wife.

4. Provisions relating to the beginning of initial repayments after completion of studies and after years of service in the armed forces or in national service programs would resemble those in existing legislation. There would also be provision for deferral of payments during any periods of exceptionally low income.

5. The bank would be authorized to enter into an agreement

with the Department of the Treasury under which the Internal Revenue Service (IRS) would undertake all collections, or, alternatively, the bank would be responsible for all collections except those that are seriously delinquent, which would be turned over to the IRS.

6. The interest rate charged the borrower would be set at a level adequate to permit the bank to obtain the funds.

7. There would be no needs test and no subsidization of interest. Interest payments would be deferred while a student was enrolled, and accrued interest obligations would become a part of the debt at the beginning of the repayment period.

8. There would be no cancellation of indebtedness for entering particular professions. Any remaining indebtedness would be cancelled upon the death of the borrower or at the end of 30 years from the date of first payment.

Unlike full contingency loan programs, such as the proposed Educational Opportunity Bank, this program does not involve redistribution of income through differing levels of repayments for individuals with different levels of income. Lower-income borrowers would have to repay their entire debt but would be able to spread repayments over a longer period. The program is modeled to some extent after the well-established Swedish student loan program, but differs from that program in some details.[7]

A point deserving emphasis in the NSLB proposal, in view of the concern of women over the inequities involved in the short repayment period, is the provision relating to couples filing joint tax returns. Since repayments would be related to the combined income of the husband and wife, they would automatically go down if the wife left the labor force for a period.

The possibility of gradually converting the Student Loan Marketing Association (SLMA or Sallie Mae) to an organization more closely resembling the NSLB seems promising.[8] The SLMA has had considerable success, through its role in creating

[7]For a discussion of Swedish student aid programs, see Woodhall (1978).

[8]See Hartman (1977) for more detailed discussion of such possibilities.

a secondary market for student loans, in expanding available loan funds. However, it would be necessary to change the status of SLMA from a profit-making to a nonprofit institution in order for it to perform the role we envisage for a NSLB, and there would have to be a number of other changes in its charter.

In some of the debates over NSLB proposals, there has been a tendency to assume that establishment of such a facility would mean an enormous increase in student borrowing and encourage institutions of higher education to raise tuition as a result. We do not believe that such fears are justified. Establishment of an NSLB would improve access to loans and reduce inequities in the student loan market, but, especially in view of the substantial amounts of grant and work-study assistance now available, there is little reason to believe that the total amount of student borrowing would rise suddenly and sharply as a result of establishment of an NSLB.[9] It might even go down because of higher interest rates and less chance to default.

Our NSLB proposal differs in some very important respects from the Tuition Advance Fund (TAF) proposed by President John Silber of Boston University and incorporated in bills introduced in Congress by Representative Michael Harrington and Senator Edward Kennedy, although there are some superficial resemblances. Under the TAF plan students (other than freshmen) could borrow to meet the costs of education. Repayments would be at the rate of 2 percent of adjusted gross income per year, with total repayment liabilities amounting to 1.5 times the original amount borrowed. As Breneman (1978, p. 62) has pointed out, to the extent that students borrowed their full costs of education, parents would be relieved of all responsibility for financing their children's education, and the principle of need-based student aid would be abandoned. Moreover, both Breneman and Dresch (1978) point out that the repayment plan would involve very heavy government subsidization of the costs

---

[9] This problem was discussed at a conference arranged by Senator Henry Bellmon of Oklahoma in Washington, D.C., on November 10, 1978. Senator Bellmon is the author of S. 3403, introduced in August 1978, which would establish a NSLB along the lines of Carnegie Council proposals.

of the program—a subsidy that would vary directly with the amount borrowed.

Recommendation 13: *Congress should give careful considera-tion to phasing out the NDSL and GSL programs and replacing them by a National Student Loan Bank (NSLB). The possibility of changes in the provisions governing the Student Loan Mar-keting Association (SLMA) to transform it into an institution resembling the proposed NSLB may well facilitate such a move.*

Provision for Part-Time Students (Including Adults)

One of the striking developments of the last decade or so has been a pronounced increase in part-time enrollment, especially among persons who are older than the traditional age of college attendance. Most of these part-time students are employed and no longer dependent on their parents. Relatively few of them apply for student aid, but those who do must be enrolled at least half time and are usually eligible for aid only on a pro-rated basis—that is, a half-time student would be eligible for only one half of the aid available to a full-time student. This implies a larger earnings expectation for part-time students that is clearly justified in most situations. For those part-time stu-dents who are independent and have dependent family mem-bers, the adjustments of earnings expectations discussed earlier would apply.

Increasingly, tuition costs of adult employed students are paid by their employers under "out-service" training programs. Such employer expenditures are tax-exempt, but only if the program of study is job-related. In the United States, in contrast with the situation in some European countries that have devel-oped paid educational leave programs, employer-financed train-ing programs of this type are often confined to white-collar em-ployees who are in line for promotion to supervisorial posi-tions.[10] We believe that there is a case for gradual development

---

[10]For an extensive analysis of paid educational leave programs in Europe, see von Moltke and Schneevoigt (1977). A recent report issued by the National Manpower Institute (1978) indicates that many tuition aid programs available for employees (under union contracts) in the United States are not utilized.

of a more general paid educational leave program that would be designed to encourage lifelong patterns of learning.

Recommendation 14: *Student aid should be available for part-time students on a pro-rated basis, provided they are enrolled for at least half-time study. In exceptional cases, where, for example, employment opportunities are impaired, the individual is handicapped, or an enrolled parent is responsible for child care, aid should be granted to students enrolled for less than half time at the discretion of the student aid officer, taking advantage of the Basic Grant override and SEOG funds.*

Future development of student aid policies for adult and part-time college students should be carefully considered in relation to the need to encourage a more general program of paid educational leave.

Simplification

One of the most common bases of complaint about student aid relates to the complexity of procedures and of federal regulations. Our recommendations aim at the development of relatively uniform and objective policies for handling most student aid applicants, leaving decisions relating to students in exceptional circumstances to the discretion of the student aid officer. Such decisions would relate, for example, to students having special difficulties in meeting earnings expectations or those meriting treatment as independent students even though they do not meet the more objective criteria we suggest in determining who is an independent student.

Among other proposals, our recommendation for a National Student Loan Bank would greatly simplify the federal role in administering student loans, compared with the present complex situation. A requirement that student aid officers would have to certify loan applications would relate the loan program more closely to the student's legitimate needs for borrowing than does the present loosely structured situation.

Some critics undoubtedly will argue that our policies imply too much delegation of responsibility to student aid officers. We would reply that student aid officers are almost universally responsible and conscientious and are usually in a better position to assess a student's special needs than federal officials, since they have more complete information about contributions to the student's expenses from all sources, including the student's earnings, his or her parents, and aid from grants or loans. There are, on the other hand, some student aid officers who do not meet these standards and who are in need of training and upgrading.

Recommendation 15: *Federal rules and regulations relating to student aid are in need of simplification, which could be accomplished by adopting our proposals, which call for more uniform and objective policies relating to most student aid applicants, leaving decisions relating to the more complex and difficult cases to student aid officers. The Office of Education should also encourage adequate training and upgrading of student aid officers.*

Increasing Emphasis on Student Aid Packaging

The U.S. Office of Education (OE) has tended to administer individual student aid programs without much consideration of their interrelationships or of the need to devote more attention to the student aid package. Recently, in recognition of growing problems with student aid programs, and especially with loan programs, OE has begun to give greater consideration to the need to restructure its policies (including proposing legislative changes where necessary) so that they result in more equitable and carefully developed student aid packages for needy students.

Nowhere has the absence of careful student aid packaging been more apparent than in the case of loans, especially under the GSL program, for those students who were not eligible for an interest subsidy and did not necessarily come in contact with a student aid officer.

We believe that the NSLB would have to depend on certification by student aid officers (probably through regional or state offices) in order to enforce a reasonable requirement that a student could not borrow more than his or her total education costs *less* any grant or Work-Study aid received and *less* the normal earnings expectation, where the self-help expectation is through earnings. Such a policy, carried out in a uniform national manner, would contribute a great deal to an accessible student loan program that also would be coherently linked to all other student aid programs. Increased attention by OE to student aid packaging would also contribute to bringing about a more equitable and structured relationship between state and federal student aid programs.

Recommendation 16: *The U.S. Office of Education should develop policies and procedures that encourage equitable and consistent student aid packages for all students, rather than treating each student aid program as a separate entity.*

Social Security Benefits for Students

The program extending social security benefits to college students aged 18 to 21 who are children of deceased, disabled, or retired workers provided valuable benefits when it was adopted in 1965, but its usefulness has become highly questionable as a result of the development of other student aid programs. In 1965, there was no federal student grant program, except for a new program (now SEOG), that was being adopted under the provisions of the Higher Education Act of 1965. It could readily be shown that dependent children who would be entitled to continuation of social security benefits under the amendment to the Social Security Act tended to come from relatively low-income families and encountered relatively severe financial barriers to participation in higher education. Moreover, the majority of industrial countries had similar provisions in their social security programs.

The case for special social security benefits is now much weaker because most of the students who receive social security benefits can qualify, on the basis of family income, for Basic Grants and other types of student aid. In fact, partly because continuation of social security benefits does not actually augment family income in many instances (especially where total family benefits are held down by the ceiling on family benefits), and partly because the total family income of a beneficiary family is treated like that of any other family in determining the expected parental contribution under the Basic Grant program, a large proportion of students receiving social security benefits qualify for full or partial Basic Grants and also for other types of student aid, including state scholarships. Thus, the additional cost of student aid resulting from elimination of the special program for social security benefits would be much smaller than the estimated saving to the Old Age Survivors and Disability Insurance (OASDI) trust fund, while certain inequities associated with the social security benefits for students would be eliminated. These inequities take the following forms: (1) some, though a relatively small minority, of those now qualifying for social security benefits would not qualify for other types of student aid under existing parental contribution schedules; and (2) the social security benefits a student actually receives vary directly with family income (instead of inversely as under other student aid programs), because the student's benefit amount is related to the earnings of the deceased, retired, or disabled worker. In addition, financing of social security benefits for students from the OASDI trust fund adds to the problem of maintaining the future solvency of that fund and involves a method of financing that is regressive.

Recommendation 17: *The Council recommends the elimination of social security benefits for college students aged 18 to 21 who are children of deceased, disabled, or retired workers.*

Food Stamps for College Students

If our proposal to meet the subsistence costs of needy students through the Basic Grant program is adopted, there would no longer be a case for food stamp benefits for college students. Even a student living at home in a family receiving public assistance would be in a position to reimburse his or her family for any loss in food stamp benefits resulting from denial of benefits to students.

Meanwhile, the policy of providing food stamps for college students, though increasingly subject to restrictive provisions, creates inequities and complexities. Perhaps most seriously, it exacerbates the problems posed by the independent student, who may in some cases be receiving food stamps even though, on the basis of parental income, he or she would not qualify for such benefits.

Finally, we believe, along with many social scientists, that provision of cash assistance to the needy, to be expended in accordance with the recipients' own needs, is far preferable to a program that subsidizes particular types of expenditures. As the President's Commission on Income Maintenance Programs put it: The Food Stamp and Commodity Distribution program, unlike other in-kind programs, could be replaced easily by a well-designed cash transfer plan. These programs supplement incomes but do so much less efficiently and with less consumer choice than direct cash transfer programs (*Poverty Amid Plenty,* 1969, p. 72).

Recommendation 18: *The Council recommends that college students no longer be eligible for food stamps.*

Summing Up: Who Does What?

THE ADMINISTRATION AND THE CONGRESS

- The Administration recommends and Congress adopts our proposed recommendations relating to the Basic Grant, CWS, SEOG, SSIG, and loan programs.

THE STATES

- The states revise their student aid legislation, where necessary, to conform to the policies we recommend relating to amounts of tuition grants, elimination of subsistence provisions in student grants, the parental contribution schedule, and portability of grants. States cannot be forced to change their legislation, of course, but they would not receive federal matching funds for amounts of aid more generous than our policies allow, and they would not receive extra matching for portable grants unless they made the relevant changes in their legislation, where necessary.

THE U.S. OFFICE OF EDUCATION

- Revises regulations to simplify procedures
- Tightens enforcement procedures to prevent abuse
- Places more emphasis on student aid packaging rather than on individual programs in developing policies and procedures
- Cooperates with institutions and associations in providing special training programs for student aid officers

INSTITUTIONS OF HIGHER EDUCATION

- Grant recognition to the importance of the functions of the student aid officer by upgrading his or her status, providing adequate staff, and making provision for participation of student aid officers in conferences and training programs
- Cooperate with federal and state agencies in making certain that institutional student aid policies conform to national policies, that students do not abuse aid programs, and that borrowers meet their repayment obligations, especially under the NDSL program (even if it is abolished, as we recommend, there will be outstanding NDSL loans for many years to come).

Glossary

Basic Grant program (BEOG): The federal Basic Educational Opportunity Grant program, enacted in 1972.

CSS: The College Scholarship Service of the College Entrance Examination Board or its "need analysis" systems.

CSS/ACT: The equivalent "need analysis" systems now used by the College Scholarship Service and the American College Testing Service. Also called "the consensus model" and "the uniform methodology."

College Work-Study (CWS): See Work-Study.

Contribution rate: The percentage of income or assets net of exemptions and other deductions which parents or students are expected to pay toward cost of attendance according to some particular system of need analysis.

Cost of attendance: The total educational expenses of a student, that is, the sum of instructional costs (tuition and fees) and noninstructional costs (room, board, books, supplies, clothing, necessary transportation, and incidentals).

Discretionary aid: Aid given students not as a matter of right but because they are judged (usually by a student aid officer) to need it in their special circumstances.

Earnings expectation: The amount a student is presumed to be able to contribute toward educational expenses from summer vacation or term-time wages.

Entitlement: A definite amount of financial assistance to which a student has a legal right.

Equal access: Equality in the ability of students from families of different incomes to pay for minimum or greater costs of higher education when student aid is taken into account.

Exemption: An amount of income or assets from which a parent or student is not expected to make any contribution toward college expenses. For dependent students the amount is what is estimated as necessary to meet subsistence costs of other family members. Termed "standard maintenance allowance" in the CSS/ACT need analysis system and "family size offset" in the Basic Grant system.

Expected family contribution: The sum of a student's expected parental contribution and his or her own expected "self-help" contribution, if any is assessed in a particular student aid program.

Expected parental contribution: The amount that parents are estimated to be able to contribute to a child's college expenses from their income and assets. In a "need-based" student aid program, aid is not allowed to take the place of a contribution of this amount.

GSL (Guaranteed Student Loan): A loan insured against default by the federal government and accorded federal interest subsidies under any of several qualifying federal, state, and private programs.

Income groups: The terms *lower income, lower-middle income, upper-middle income,* and *upper income* are used in accordance with Table 5.

Independent student: A student whose parents are not expected to contribute financially toward meeting his or her educational expenses.

Means test: A system of "need analysis" for determining the amount that a student's parents are able to pay toward college expenses, and thereby whether the student qualifies for "need-based" aid.

Table 5. Explanation of terms for describing income groups

	Refers to members of families with income in the:	Income range (1979 est.)	Percent of all families	Percent of families in income bracket with young people aged 18 to 24	Percent of families in income bracket with young people enrolled in college full-time
Lower income	lowest quartile for all families	less than $10,600	25%	22%	12%
Lower middle income	second quartile for all families	$10,600 to $18,500	25	20	15
Upper middle income	third quartile for all families	$18,500 to $27,800	25	22	22
Upper income	highest quartile for all families	$27,800 or more	25	36	51
		Total:	100%	100%	100%

MISAA: The federal Middle-Income Student Assistance Act of 1978.

NDSL: The federal National Direct Student Loan program, the successor to the National Defense Student Loan program of the same acronym.

NSLB: A National Student Loan Bank having the principal features proposed by the Carnegie Council and by the Carnegie Commission before it.

Need analysis: A "means-test" method for estimating the ability of families to pay college expenses.

Need-based aid: Student aid awarded to fill the gap between the "expected family contribution" of a student and the student's costs of attendance.

Noninstructional costs: That part of "costs of attendance" representing room, board, books, supplies, clothing, necessary transportation, and incidentals.

Packaging: The approach to making student aid awards under which several different sources of aid funds are drawn upon in order to provide a student with a total amount of aid equal to the difference between the student's "cost of attendance" and "family contribution."

Sallie Mae (SLMA): The Student Loan Marketing Association, a financial institution chartered by Congress in 1972 to provide lenders in the GSL program with an opportunity to sell GSL loans or to obtain advances by offering such loans as security. Analogous to the Federal National Mortgage Association ("Fannie Mae"); hence the similar acronym.

SEOG: The federal Supplemental Educational Opportunity Grant program, the successor to the former Educational Opportunity Grant (EOG) program, renamed in 1972 to distinguish it from the Basic Educational Opportunity Grant program.

SSIG: The federal State Student Incentive Grant program enacted in 1972 or the "need-based" state scholarship and grant programs that are eligible for federal matching funds under the 1972 legislation.

Work-Study (W-S): The federal Work-Study program that allocates federal funds to colleges and universities to pay 80 percent of the wages of students. Sometimes referred to as *College Work-Study.*

Part Two

The Current System in Operation

3

The Growth of
Student Aid Funds

The increase in the commitment of public funds to student aid programs has been the most remarkable development in public support for higher education in the last decade. The public share of student aid from all sources shifted correspondingly— from about two thirds at the beginning of the decade to almost 90 percent currently (Figure 7).

Federal Student Aid

Federally financed aid to undergraduate students is largely a phenomenon of the last two decades. Except for a work-study program under the auspices of the National Youth Administration during the Great Depression of the 1930s, the only major federal program of student aid before 1958 was that provided for veterans under the G.I. Bill of Rights, enacted in 1944.

The greatest growth in student aid has occurred in the 1970s. In just the four-year period from fiscal years 1974 to 1978, the total sum involved in federal student aid programs, exclusive of veterans' benefits, increased from $1.8 billion to $4.9 billion (Table 6). Even in constant (1972) dollars, this total more than doubled. In 1979-80, such federal funds will amount to more than $6 billion. If veterans' benefits, which reached their peak in 1975-76 and have since been declining (as Vietnam era veterans move into older age brackets) are in-

Figure 7. Student aid expenditures from federal, state, and private sources, fiscal years 1960 to 1980 (in billions of current and constant 1972 dollars)

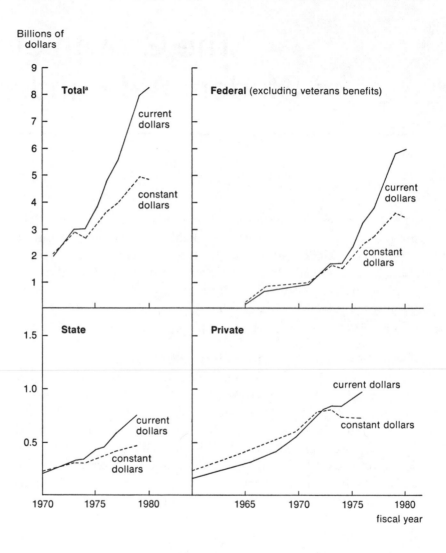

[a]Estimated, 1977 to 1980.

Source: Tables 6 to 8.

Table 6. Federal outlays for selected student aid programs, selected fiscal years, 1965 to 1980
(in millions of current and constant 1972 dollars)

Fiscal year[a]	Basic Grants	SEOG	Work-Study	Loan programs[b]	SSIG program	Social security benefits	Total Current dollars	Total Constant dollars	Benefits for veterans
			U.S. Department of Health, Education, and Welfare Programs						
1965			55.7	160.1			215.8	288.5	
1967		112.0	134.1	238.0		256.0	740.1	940.4	43.0
1969		124.6	139.9	230.7		366.0	861.2	1,008.4	275.9
1971		167.7	158.4	231.7		455.0	1,012.8	1,068.4	590.0
1973		210.9	270.2	685.7		638.0	1,804.8	1,750.5	1,117.3
1974	49.0	211.4	271.1	620.0	19.0	618.0	1,788.5	1,595.5	2,016.0
1975	342.0	240.3	300.2	680.0	20.0	840.0	2,422.5	1,964.7	2,309.0
1976	905.0	241.9	525.0	619.0	42.7	998.0	3,331.6	2,516.3	3,479.0
1977	1,387.0	252.8	437.4	589.0	62.1	1,181.0	3,909.3	2,782.4	4,301.0
1978	2,140.0	270.1	435.0	805.3	64.0	1,227.0	4,941.4	3,287.7	2,697.0
1979	2,600.0	340.1	550.0	1,030.7	63.8	1,378.0	5,962.6	3,701.2	2,214.0
1980	2,444.0	340.1	550.0	1,194.4	76.8	1,509.0	6,114.3	3,546.6	1,892.0

[a]Amounts for fiscal years prior to 1978 are actual outlays; amounts for fiscal years 1978 and 1979 are estimated outlays; amounts for 1980 are those in the administration budget. The Consumer Price Index for 1978-79 and 1979-80 has been estimated.

[b]Includes appropriations for NDSL program plus interest subsidies and cost of defaults in GSL program.

Sources: Carnegie Council on Policy Studies in Higher Education (1975, Table 4); *Special Analyses, Budget of the U.S. Government* (selected years); *The Budget of the U.S. Government* (selected years); and Fields (1979).

cluded, the total involved in federal student aid in 1979-80 is likely to be in the neighborhood of $8.0 billion.

The federal role in student aid at first evolved slowly. The successful launching of Sputnik by the Soviet Union in 1957, with its implications for U.S. progress in scientific achievement, led to enactment of the National Defense Education Act of 1958, which provided for a program of federally funded loans to needy students (now known as the National Direct Student Loan program—NDSL), as well as for graduate fellowships and for grants to state and local school systems for programs to improve instruction in mathematics and the sciences.

The 1960s were characterized by a new wave of concerns stimulated by the civil rights movement and the related anti-poverty program. The Economic Opportunity Act of 1964 included a provision for the College Work-Study program, under which the federal government paid 90 percent of the earnings of needy students who were provided jobs on the campus or in nonprofit off-campus organizations. The normal federal share is now 80 percent. The enactment of the Higher Education Act of 1965 marked the beginning of a broad-ranging program of federal aid to higher education, with substantial emphasis on aid to low-income students under provisions for (1) Educational Opportunity Grants (now the Supplemental Educational Opportunity Grant program—SEOG), (2) the federally insured student loan program (now known as the Guaranteed Student Loan program—GSL), and (3) incorporation of the Work-Study program into the new legislative authorizations. In the same year, the Social Security Act was amended to permit continued payments of benefits to deceased, disabled, or retired workers' children aged 18 to 21 who were enrolled in school or college.

By the latter part of the 1960s, a number of federal legislative provisions for different types of student aid, with major emphasis on assistance to needy students, were in place. But the overall impact of federal student aid programs was very limited. Not only did the sums available fall far short of the need of students for aid, but there were also serious inequities in the way in which federal funds were allocated to institutions of higher education.

Another way of describing the problem is that federal student aid provisions fell short of providing for "entitlement" to aid. A needy student could not be assured of receiving assistance, not only because of the inadequacy of available funds, but also because the funds appropriated under three major student aid programs—the so-called campus-based programs (EOG, CWS, and NDSL)—were allocated to institutions of higher education rather than to students. Each institution then chose the ultimate recipients.

As Congress approached the 1972 amendments to higher education legislation, a major debate over federal aid to higher education got underway. Among associations representing institutions of higher education, and among some members of congressional committees concerned with federal education legislation, there was, on the one hand, strong support for a new federal program of institutional aid to higher education that would allocate to each institution an amount that would be directly related to the number of students enrolled, according to one or another of several proposed formulas. On the other hand, some congressional leaders and some private organizations, including the Carnegie Commission on Higher Education, were opposed to across-the-board institutional aid, arguing that the cornerstone of federal aid to higher education should consist of a far more adequate program of aid to needy students than yet existed.

The most important innovation of the Education Amendments of 1972 was the Basic Educational Opportunity Grant (Basic Grant) program. It was designed as an "entitlement" program. That is, the discretionary award procedures under which each institution determined which students would receive aid under the "campus-based" programs would not apply. Family resources and cost of attendance alone would determine who received a Basic Grant and in what amount. However, in the first few years after enactment of the Basic Grant legislation, amounts appropriated for the program fell far short of the sums that would have been required for true entitlement. But, as Table 6 indicates, the amounts expended increased sharply from 1974-75 on, and grants began to approach the amounts contemplated in the 1972 legislation and to have a major impact on the total amount of aid available for needy students.

Another important addition to federal student aid programs under the 1972 Amendments was the State Student Incentive Grant program (SSIG), which provided for federal funds to match, on a 50-50 basis, increases in student aid appropriations by states. This provision has been effective in inducing states that did not previously have need-based student aid programs to adopt them, but the amounts appropriated, though gradually increasing, have fallen far short of those that would be required for a well-designed and carefully coordinated federal-state system of student aid.

State Student Aid

Many early state student aid programs were designed to assist students of superior ability, and only gradually states began to design programs in which eligibility was based primarily on need.[1] In 1969-70, the first year in which comprehensive data on state student aid programs were gathered, there were 19 states that had need-based undergraduate scholarship or grant programs, providing aid to 470,000 students and representing state appropriations of almost $200 million. By 1978-79 a total of 57 states and territories had some type of state student aid program, aiding nearly 1.2 million students and expending $828.9 million—$765.1 million in state funds and $63.8 in federal matching funds (Tables 6 and 7).

The scope of aid programs varies enormously from state to state. In some, academic criteria of selection are retained; in others, they are not. State programs also vary greatly in their relative impact on students in public and private institutions. Some programs are designed to channel most of the aid to students in private institutions. At the other extreme, there are a few states that, often because of restrictions in their state constitutions, limit aid to students enrolled in public institutions.

[1] For a more extensive discussion of state student aid programs, see Carnegie Council (1977).

Table 7. Dollar awards of state-funded, need-based undergraduate
scholarship/grant programs (in millions of current and constant
1972 dollars)[a]

| | Dollar awards | |
Academic year	Current dollars	Constant dollars
1969-70	$199.9	$221.4
1970-71	236.3	249.3
1971-72	268.6	273.0
1972-73	315.5	306.0
1973-74	345.2	307.9
1974-75	420.8	341.3
1975-76	467.5	373.1
1976-77	589.3	419.4
1977-78	673.0	449.8
1978-79	765.1	474.9

[a]Does not include federal SSIG funds.

Source: National Association of State Scholarship and Grant Programs (1978).

Student Aid from Private Sources

Despite the enormous increase in public funds available for student aid, private initiative continues to play a significant role. We estimate that total funds for student aid stemming from the predominantly private sources included in Table 8 amounted to nearly $1 billion in 1975-76. They are probably even larger today.

One of the striking findings of the Council's survey of private institutions summarized in *The States and Private Higher Education* (1977, Appendix C) was that student aid from discretionary internal resources continued to increase from 1970-71 to 1975-76, both in states that had substantial state scholarship programs and in states that had only minimal programs. Of campuses responding to a 1978 Council survey, 62 percent say they allocate unrestricted revenues to provide fee waivers or grants to students. Of this number, 27 percent say that the dollar value of such financial aid has risen faster than

Table 8. Student aid revenue of institutions of higher education from
private sources, student aid deficits of institutions, and direct private aid
to students, 1959-60 to 1975-76
(in millions of current and constant 1972 dollars)

Year	Student aid revenue— private sources[a]	Student aid deficits[b]	Direct private aid (estimated)[c]	Total Current dollars	Total Constant dollars
1959-60	$ 67.9	$ 79.8	$23.2	$170.9	$243.4
1961-62	85.9	111.0	27.1	224.0	311.5
1963-64	100.7	152.6	30.4	283.7	384.9
1965-66	141.8	166.9	37.8	346.5	452.9
1967-68	173.9	214.8	40.7	429.4	526.9
1969-70	230.0	300.0	43.3	573.3	634.9
1970-71	273.0	380.0	48.0	701.0	739.5
1971-72	262.9	475.3	55.9	794.1	807.0
1972-73	276.0	522.3	60.1	858.4	832.6
1973-74	281.1	513.9	65.0	860.0	767.2
1974-75	283.9 (est)	568.4 (est)	73.3	925.6	750.7
1975-76	286.7 (est)	628.5 (est)	81.7	996.9	752.9

[a]Includes private gifts and grants for student aid, endowment income restricted to student aid, and "other student aid grants." Data for the latter two items are no longer available.

[b]Total institutional expenditures for student aid less total institutional revenue for student aid. Data on revenue for student aid are no longer available from reports of the U.S. National Center for Education Statistics and must be estimated from scattered sources.

[c]Includes aid provided directly to students by business firms, churches, and so on. Following the procedure in Carnegie Commission on Higher Education (1973, p. 134), it is assumed to amount to 1 percent of total tuition and fee revenue.

Sources: Carnegie Commission on Higher Education (1973, Table A-14); U.S. National Center for Education Statistics, selected publications; and other sources.

gross tuition over the last decade. Twelve percent of those allocating such funds say such aid is used "to a large extent" to meet the needs of students not eligible under conventional need analyses; an additional 31 percent mention that this is true "to some extent."

This growth in internally generated student aid represents the emergence of a multiple pricing system, primarily in private higher education but perhaps to some extent in public higher education as well. Some students, chiefly those from more affluent families, pay full tuition, while many students who receive scholarships pay a reduced proportion of the full rate, the reduction depending on the size of that portion of the aid package financed by the college's own unrestricted funds. The sharp tuition increases that have been made necessary by the inflationary trends of the 1970s have typically been adopted by private colleges and universities with full recognition of the fact that—for a substantial proportion of students—it would be necessary to increase student aid awards from internal sources in order to offset the burden of the increase in tuition on less affluent students.

In some of these situations, the effect of the multiple pricing system may be that the more affluent students who pay full tuition are meeting part of the cost of scholarships for less affluent students. Even in those institutions in which tuition revenue meets only a portion of educational costs and the college's own scholarships are normally financed from endowment and gift funds, the added revenue from a portion of a tuition increase may be allocated to provide additional student aid. It is apparent that this practice has been growing in the competitive atmosphere of the 1970s and is likely to become even more important when the college-age population declines in size in the 1980s and competition for students—or, in the more selective institutions, for the most desired students—becomes even more intense.

The total institutional student aid deficits (student aid expenditures less revenues earmarked for aid) provide a rough measure of the extent of multiple pricing. As Table 8 shows, such pricing is a large and rapidly growing source of student aid funds. Although most of the total reflects funds from private sources, in the case of public institutions of higher education student aid deficits may be funded partly from public sources.[2]

[2]Unfortunately, precise data on the total student aid deficit of institutions are no longer available because, after 1973-74, the financial statistics collected by the U.S. National Center for Education Statistics no longer identified revenue received for student aid as a separate item in institutional accounts. We have developed estimates drawn from a variety of federal, state, and other sources.

Student Aid from All Sources

Tables 6 to 8 suggest the overall magnitude of resources flowing into student aid, but they should be read with certain considerations in mind. First, the amount of loan funds available to students is not accurately indicated by annual appropriations for the GSL or NDSL programs. In the former case, the appropriations represent the costs of federal subsidies to the program, while in the latter the annual appropriation augments revolving funds already available to institutions. Judging from data gathered by the American Council on Education, total borrowing under the National Direct Student Loan and Guaranteed Student Loan programs (including borrowing by graduate students) amounted to about $1.5 billion in 1976-77 (Atelsek and Gomberg, 1977).

Taking these considerations into account and allowing for small amounts of aid not included at all in Tables 6 to 8 (for example, certain graduate fellowship programs), it can be estimated that the total amount of funds flowing into student aid chiefly for undergraduates reached about $5.5 billion in 1976-77 and will come to about $8 billion in 1979-80, not including veterans' benefits (Figure 7). Adding in veterans' benefits, the amounts are even greater.

The increases, of course, have been much less pronounced in constant dollars. The problem of attempting to keep up with inflation since the oil crisis of 1973-74 is vividly portrayed in Figure 7. While the rise in federal and state funds was substantial even after adjustment for inflation, the estimated flow of private funds leveled off after 1971-72.

Tax Exemptions

Thus far, we have been discussing direct student aid. To round out the review, we need to take account of the effect of tax exemptions and deductions that benefit students and their families. These include federal income tax exemptions for dependent students, exemption of fellowships and scholarships from federal income taxes, exclusion of veterans' and social security benefits, and exemptions under state income tax provisions. Other types of tax exemptions benefiting higher education, such as tax deductions for philanthropic contributions, do not necessarily benefit students and their families and thus should not be counted as additive to student aid resources. The total value of exemptions affecting students and their families has been estimated at approximately $1 billion in 1976-77 (Congressional Budget Office, 1978a, Table 1). This amount would have been very substantially increased if tuition tax credit legislation had been adopted by Congress in 1978.

Conclusion

Perhaps the most striking aspect of the growth of student aid is the pronounced acceleration in the 1970s of the longer-term increase in public funds made available for student aid purposes. Increases have been especially large since fiscal year 1974, that is, during a period when enrollment in higher education was not growing nearly as rapidly as in the 1960s. An important part of the explanation, of course, is the high rate of inflation in the 1970s, which has forced colleges and universities, both public and private, to adopt substantial increases in tuition and other charges and created pressure for offsetting increases in both public and private student aid allocations.

But it is clear that inflation has not been the only influence at work. Spokesmen for minority groups, the student lobby, the higher education associations, and other organizations have been effective in impressing Congress with the need to increase student aid appropriations. The impact of high interest rates and the cost of defaults have been significant influences on appropriations for the Guaranteed Student Loan program. Moreover, in 1978 pressure for relief for middle-income families became a powerful force in stimulating Congressional support for tuition tax credits, which were almost adopted, and for the Middle-Income Student Assistance Act, which was enacted.

4

Need Analysis

It is not possible to get very far in a discussion of any aspect of student aid without coming upon questions about how student need is to be measured. The traditional phrase for such measures is *means test*. Students of public policy usually speak of *income tests*. Student aid officers usually speak of *need analysis* or *family contribution schedules*. Whatever terminology is used, two things are at issue: how much the student and the student's family can be expected to pay and how much an educational program costs. The difference between these two is "need."

In any set of student aid programs that award funds according to need, the influence of the means tests used will be pervasive. Means tests will affect:

- The distribution of aid funds among students—who gets how much
- The relative efficiency of different aid programs in creating opportunities for higher education
- The degree to which an aid system is justified in terms of differing social goals, especially equality of opportunity
- The strength of the case for financing the student aid program from public sources, in particular from taxes, which may or may not be as progressive as a means test for determining parental and student contributions toward college expenses
- The question of whether there are, or are not, enough aid funds in the aggregate—since the sum of all the "need" of

individual students is at least the most obvious criterion of
how much aid is enough
• Differences in the financial impact of aid programs on institutions with their differing mixes of low-income and high-
income students
• The financial implications of differences in status among students—whether, for the purpose of determining their need for
aid, they are dependent or self-supporting, single or married,
part-time or full-time, graduates or undergraduates

Need analysis is also a very complex subject. Like the law
in general or the tax system in particular, the rules laid down
for any need analysis system are then applied to cases which are
infinitely various. A conscientious wish to be just and fair can
rapidly lead to a proliferation of subordinate rules and provisos
that take this variety more and more into account. The increasing entrance of public officials into the need analysis field in the
1970s often resulted in relatively simple systems for particular
federal or state programs, but they were additional systems
that often drew different distinctions between families' ability
to pay than those of the private organizations, thus increasing
the total complexity of need analysis.

The complexity of some systems of need analysis suggests
that the ability of families to pay for education can be determined with some precision. This is far from being the case. The
question of how much a family should be expected to give for
education is, in the end, a question of what they should be expected to give up. All the decisions that go into what econ-
omists think of as consumer preferences therefore have a bearing on the validity of a means test. What standard of housing or
eating or clothing or recreation should a family of given income
be expected to forego in order to finance the education of their
offspring? What are necessities and what are luxuries? Which
outlays are "discretionary" and which are not? How can ability
to pay for education be distinguished from willingness to pay?

Further, there are, at best, only limited possibilities of
empirically testing judgments about these questions. No matter
how demanding a means test, there will be at least a few fami-

lies with any given income who are willing to undertake the sacrifices necessary to make the financial contributions the test expects of them, or more. No matter how lax the test, there will be at least a few families who are unwilling, and who constrain the opportunities of their offspring accordingly. The most one can perhaps say is that a means test is about right if under it most families at each level of income could not provide, by practicing routine economies, much more financial support than that expected of them.

The mechanism of most means tests is like that of the federal income tax system: Rates of contribution are applied to what is left of income or assets after exempting and deducting specified amounts. Some exemptions are standardized, among them allowances for the ordinary living expenses of members of the family other than the student but also including such items as reserves for emergencies or the retirement of the parents. Other deductions allow for actual expenses incurred, such as medical expenses or the costs of educating members of the family other than the aid applicant.

A mechanism paralleling the income tax system in this way is desirable because it is widely understood in our society. However, much depends on the precise features of a particular scheme. Rates of contribution that increase with higher levels of income are progressive and result in contributions that amount to higher percentages of income for higher-income families. But high standard exemptions or deductions can affect, in much the same way, the relative contributions of families with incomes exceeding the standard amounts. In general, a system of need analysis that is relatively generous in its exemptions and relatively demanding in its contribution rates does more for lower-middle income students than one which has low exemptions and low contribution rates.

Need analysis has been by no means static. The College Scholarship Service (CSS), a private organization affiliated with the College Entrance Examination Board, originated its system in the 1950s and has modified it frequently ever since. The American College Testing Service (ACT) has also changed its system from time to time and so have state student aid agencies and the federal Basic Grants program. Each version of each system has been internally consistent, and in that sense fair, but their differing results raise questions of equity among families.

The versions of the CSS need analysis system that were in use by the late 1950s were quite demanding. In the 1950s, when the CSS was founded, a lower-income or lower-middle-income family wanting a college education for its children might feel compelled to refinance a home or business to raise the necessary cash. Such families might decide to send only their brightest to college, or only their male children. Parents and relatives often loaned students money from savings accumulated for retirement. Some especially cohesive families would work out an understanding that the children would take turns going to college, with the children not in college at a particular time taking jobs and contributing to the expenses of a brother or sister who was enrolled. Such efforts were being made at a time when real incomes generally were far lower than today.

The early versions of the CSS system should be viewed against this background. They resulted in expected family contributions considerably higher and from families of lower real incomes than the need analysis systems most in use today. At a time when so many families were making heroic sacrifices to send children to college, a demanding test of whether families had reached the limit of their ability to pay for education must have seemed appropriate.

In the late 1960s the CSS, with its increasingly broad grass-roots membership, sensed a growing reluctance of middle-income families to make the large sacrifices expected of them in the past. Somewhat haltingly at first and then dramatically in 1974, the CSS relaxed its means test for 1975-76. Figure 8 shows this more recent history of the CSS. It is worth noting that the reduction in the expected percentages of family income was roughly the same whether measured in current or in constant dollars (Table 9). It is also of considerable importance that the slope of the lines in the figure has not greatly changed. This is because the changes were accomplished mainly through increasing exemptions rather than by lowering contribution rates. Emphasis on this approach favored lower-middle-income fami-

Figure 8. Expected parental contribution for a four-member family
without special exemptions and deductions, by before-tax income, College
Scholarship Service, selected years 1973-74 to 1979-80 (current dollars)

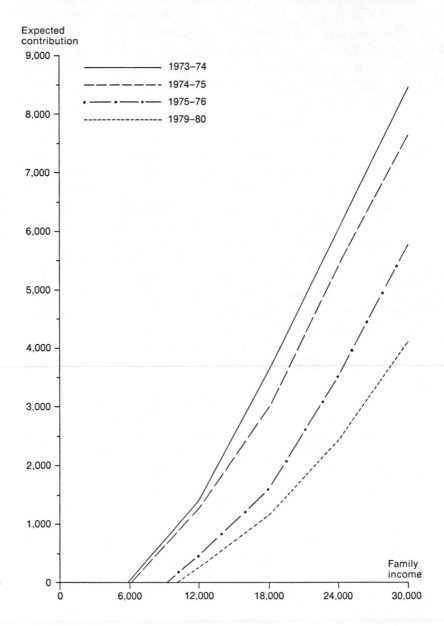

Source: Table 9.

Table 9. Changes in expected parental contributions for a four-member family, without special exemptions and deductions, by before-tax income, College Scholarship Service, selected years, 1956-57 to 1979-80 (in current dollars and constant 1978 dollars)

Year	Current dollar parental incomes and contributions					
	$6,000	$12,000	$18,000	$24,000	$30,000	$36,000
1956-57	685	1,805	a	a	a	a
1960-61	700	1,810	3,110	4,010	a	a
1965-66	580	2,080	4,150	a	a	a
1972-73	50	1,400	3,390	5,810	7,960	a
1973-74	24	1,406	3,647	6,116	8,312	a
1974-75	0	1,265	2,999	5,424	7,580	a
1975-76	0	460	1,590	3,510	5,760	7,820
1979-80	0	270	1,150	2,420	4,130	5,680
	Constant dollar parental incomes and contributions					
1956-57	623	1,334	2,095	3,167	4,501	6,047
1960-61	596	1,329	2,154	3,276	4,651	6,025
1965-66	0	1,012	2,282	3,875	5,662	7,707
1972-73	0	561	1,946	3,430	5,754	8,112
1973-74	0	522	1,904	3,832	6,324	8,798
1974-75	0	544	1,901	3,441	5,746	8,150
1975-76	0	0	934	2,072	3,832	6,053
1979-80	0	270	1,150	2,420	4,130	5,680

[a]Not shown in source tables.

Source: Annual tables of the College Scholarship Service. For constant dollar panel, 1978 incomes deflated to earlier year equivalents; corresponding contributions then inflated to 1978 dollars.

lies relatively more than upper-middle-income families, as compared with what a uniform reduction of contribution rates would have accomplished. Still, the percentage of income that even an upper-income family was expected to contribute has been reduced very substantially. Table 9 provides data on the earlier history of the CSS schedule, as well as data for more recent years.

The steps taken by CSS in 1974 to liberalize its need analysis system were quickly followed by ACT. A coalition of private organizations developed a combination of both systems and recommended that it be regarded as a "consensus model" and become the national standard for all systems as a "uniform methodology." The U.S. Office of Education went along with this suggestion to the extent of issuing regulations that require CSS and ACT and all new private providers of need analysis computations to reach results like those CSS reached in 1976-77 academic year in standard family situations and subject only to adjustments for inflation.

One of the effects of the liberalization of the CSS/ACT systems of assessing parental contributions has been to increase very substantially the maximum family income at which at least some student aid can be expected, in the absence of a student earnings contribution. This maximum is related to the total cost at the institution selected by the student, since the student's eligibility for assistance disappears at the point at which the expected family contribution equals total cost. Figure 9 shows how this "threshold income" increased under the CSS schedule for parents of students commuting to a public two-year college and for on-campus resident students at public four-year and private colleges.

The Basic Grant Means Test

Changes in the Basic Grant method of calculating expected parental contributions were at first much slower in coming and then even sharper in their impact, but they have been in the same direction. The earliest Basic Grant family contribution schedule was designed to produce parental contribution figures roughly equal to those that the then-applicable CSS schedule would have produced if the amount of the CSS expectation of student summer earnings had been added to that of parents and expected of them rather than of children and if the CSS expectation of a contribution from parental capital assets had been somewhat higher. As the CSS system was liberalized, the Basic Grant system remained largely unchanged and thus became relatively more demanding. For several years, changes in the Basic Grant system mainly had the effect of reducing slightly its ex-

Figure 9. Parental income at which expected parental contribution equals average student expense budgets, five-member family, College Scholarship Service, 1972-73 to 1978-79

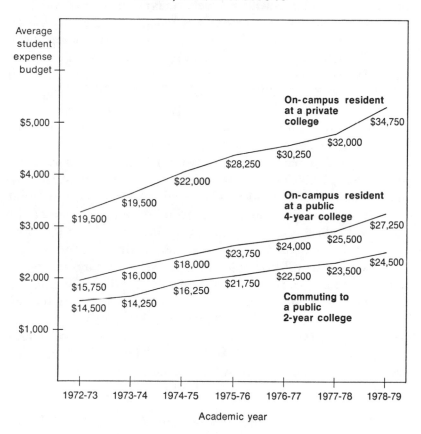

Source: Nelson and Van Dusen (1978), at the suggestion of Kenneth Deitch.

pectation of asset contributions. Then, in 1978, the Middle-Income Student Assistance Act (MISAA) reduced the rates of parental contribution drastically so that they would be substantially lower for most families with incomes over $8,000. The contribution rate is reduced to a flat 10.5 percent, compared with the former rates of 20 percent of the first $5,000 of income after exemptions and deductions and 30 percent of the excess over $5,000.

Under the new Basic Grant parental contribution schedule, as under the old, a student from a family with an annual income up to about $6,000 will receive a maximum grant, which in 1979-80 will be $1,800 (unless it is reduced by the 50-percent-of-cost limitation). For families with annual incomes above about $8,000, the expected parental contribution will be considerably smaller than under the old schedule. For families with incomes above $15,000 the parental contribution expected under the former means test generally would have exceeded the maximum grant and the student would have received no Basic Grant assistance under the old schedule. But under the new test, the expected parental contribution for families with incomes just above $15,000 will be reduced to roughly half of the former amount, and the student will be entitled to a grant of about $1,000. The family contribution will rise, and the size of the grant will fall, until, for families with incomes above $25,000, the contribution will at least equal the maximum grant and no Basic Grant aid will be available. The expected parental contribution for families with incomes up to about $18,000, assessed according to the new system, still is higher than under the liberalized CSS/ACT schedule. But above $18,000 the expected parental contribution is even lower under the new Basic Grant system than under the CSS/ACT system (Figure 9). This is because the approach of MISAA is to reduce contribution rates, rather than the CSS/ACT approach of increasing exemptions.

Appraising the Middle-Income Student Assistance Act

How should one appraise what the Congress has done? Clearly, MISAA marks another milestone in the shifting of responsibility for financing higher education from parents to public. Obviously, also, it provides lower-middle- and upper-middle-income parents with additional and welcome relief—that was its intent. But does it undermine the need-based character of the student aid system and its foundation in equal opportunity objectives? Does the new aid look more like a family allowance program for families with children in college? The answers to these questions depend in part on one's view of the new 10.5 percent contribution rate. It means that a family with an income of $25,000 is expected to provide $525 more toward educational expenses than a family, otherwise identical, with an income of $20,000. Would it be too hard for the higher-income family to find more than $525 out of the additional income by practicing routine economies?

Another way of looking at the question is to assume the Congressional premise that middle-income families needed relief from rising college costs and to ask which mechanism of providing relief is most appropriate. For reasons given in more detail in Section 9, the Congress was surely right in rejecting an across-the-board tax credit. Such a credit would have been largely self-defeating and would have allocated much of the available relief to families with incomes well above any that can reasonably be termed "middle" income. Relief through changes in means tests was more appropriate. But in choosing to emphasize reduction in need analysis contribution rates rather than an increase in exemptions, the Congress did less than it could have (at the same cost) to help lower-middle-income families. The CSS/ACT approach of increasing exemptions is more effective in concentrating additional assistance on the lower end of the middle-income range (Figure 5). It is also less arbitrary, in that an emphasis on exemptions keeps in focus the question of what contributions to education are feasible for families making reasonable economies in living standards.

The importance of need analysis to the fairness, effectiveness and administerability of the student aid system strongly suggests the desirability of a public consensus about what families should be expected to contribute toward educational expenses. The instability produced by alternative systems in recent years suggests the desirability of having a single recognized system. Coordination between federal, state, and private aid (discussed in Section 15) will continue to be extremely difficult in the absence of a single standard. At this writing, the CSS/ACT system seems the better—because the more progressive—of the major systems in use. The difference between the CSS/ACT and MISAA approaches is more pronounced the higher the family's income. In the Basic Grant program itself the difference is limited by the existence of a "cut off"—no student whose parental contribution exceeds $1,600 receives any Basic Grant aid. But if the MISAA schedule is used in determining aid under other programs that do not have a cut-off feature, it can result in aid to families with incomes of $50,000 and more. Such use is permitted by current U.S. Office of Education regulations for other federal aid programs.

5

Packaging Student Aid

The student aid officer has the task of building a "package" of resources of various kinds that will enable the individual student to meet his or her total costs. The foundation of such a structure is the student's expected family contribution. The student aid officer attempts to identify amounts of aid from other sources that will cover the expenses the student's family contri bution will not cover. In doing so, the aid officer will ordinarily seek to be fair to other students attending the particular college. The approaches designed to assure such fairness can be quite complicated. Here we will only consider what is involved in making aid from various sources match the need of the individual student.

Aid as a Matter of Right

When the student aid officer has determined the amount of family resources available for educational expenses, the next step is to determine the amount of any other aid the student will receive as a matter of right, which the student aid officer can assume as a given. The student aid officer will add the amount of such aid to the expected family contribution and subtract this total from the cost of attendance to determine the student's need for discretionary forms of aid. There are four types of aid to which large numbers of students are entitled in some formula-determined amount:

- Basic Grants
- State scholarships in most states

- G.I. Bill benefits
- Social security student benefits

Basic Grants

The Basic Grant program has been the most rapidly growing federal student aid program since 1972, when it was first enacted. If enough money has been appropriated by the Congress to provide the maximum grants authorized by law, the amount of the individual's grant is determined by a fairly simple formula. The amount is the difference between $1,800 and the student's family contribution, or one half the cost of attending the institution the student has chosen, whichever is less. For many eligible students, it is the first part of the formula that is operative and the amount of the Basic Grant is the amount required to bring the sum of family contribution and Basic Grant up to $1,800. In this sense, the Basic Grant program has a strong tendency to equalize student resources, at least up to $1,800.

For many students, the restriction that limits awards to one half of costs of attendance amounts to an implicit earnings expectation, since they must find other resources to cover the other half of costs. The restriction in practice affects only those students from families with incomes so low that a family contribution of less than about $900 is expected. All others receive the same Basic Grant whether they attend high- or low-cost institutions, because the lowest cost institution (counting both the subsistence and tuition expenses allowed by the program) costs more than twice the difference between $1,800 and their family contributions. But for the lowest income students, the amount of the Basic Grant does vary with costs, with the federal government in effect paying 50 percent of the added cost of choosing a more expensive institution, up to one costing $3,600.

The above discussion implies that the amount of a student's Basic Grant does not depend on an amount of money allocated to students from a particular state or to students attending a particular institution. This is indeed the case. Ordinarily, the federal government commits itself in a given year to pay the grant to which a student is estimated to be entitled on the basis of available appropriations no matter how many students turn out to be eligible or how large their properly computed grants. The Congress could, in principle, reduce the federal commitment for a given year by appropriating less than would be required for the aggregate of all awards under the announced "payment schedule," but the Basic Grant statute provides procedures for this that would be virtually impossible to administer.

State Grants

It is difficult to generalize about the second type of aid students sometimes receive as a matter of right—state grants—because state programs differ so widely. Some use the CSS/ACT means test, others use their own schedules of grant awards that are equivalent to means tests. Most provide grants only for students attending institutions located in the awarding state; a few provide grants that are "portable" out of state. Some provide major amounts of aid to many students, others only small awards or awards to only a few of the eligible students. What can be said in the way of generalization is that the larger and more established the state aid program, the more likely it is:

1. To make its awards primarily on the basis of financial need
2. To deal directly with students in determining their eligibility for aid
3. To make awards in amounts that are at least somewhat sensitive to the tuition charged by the institution the student attends

Since the difference in costs between colleges tends to result primarily from differences in tuition charges, these programs are often seen and advocated primarily as "tuition equalization" programs, that is, as tending to equalize the costs of attending public and private institution. However, this is a difference of emphasis only. We have seen that Basic Grant awards are sensitive to tuition costs in some cases. Some of the state grant programs play a considerable role in equalizing student resources for subsistence.

Since 1972, federal legislation has authorized the State Student Incentive Grant (SSIG) program, designed to provide an incentive—in the form of federal matching funds—for states to initiate or expand grant programs. This federal legislation requires, for a state program to be eligible, that the state base awards on need; but this requirement has been very broadly interpreted, so that almost any method for calculating need and almost any weight given need in calculating award amounts has been regarded as acceptable. There is, as a result, only a rough— and often only tenuous—complementarity between the federal Basic Grant program and the state grant programs. It has been the exception, rather than the rule, for states to adjust their eligibility rules, award amounts, cost allowances, or application deadlines to those of the federal program. However, many states now ask students applying for state aid to find out first the amount of the Basic Grant to which they are entitled.

The G.I. Bill

The Veterans "G.I. Bill" program is a third major entitlement to aid that the student aid officer looks to in building aid packages. Only students who are veterans (or certain dependents or survivors of veterans) are eligible, but if they are, the benefits are generous compared to those of any other single program. Indeed, if the veteran chooses a low-cost public institution, the student aid officer will often find that the sum of veterans benefit and Basic Grant will close the student's need gap entirely, even if the student is not expected to obtain any financial help from his parents. If the veteran is an "independent" student whose parental resources are disregarded, veterans benefits and Basic Grants are coordinated, to the extent that the veterans entitlement is treated by the Basic Grant program as income subject to the Basic Grant contribution rate. If the veteran is considered dependent, there is no coordination of benefits— neither the Basic Grant or veterans benefit is reduced because of the other.

G.I. Bill benefits are neither calculated in a way that will equalize educational resources among veterans, nor in a way that will provide larger entitlements to veterans choosing more expensive colleges. In this sense, G.I. Bill benefits are not "need based," although many veterans are in fact needy. The lack of any calculated need factor in determining a veterans benefit has had important effects on the use made of the G.I. Bill in recent years. Many veterans using the program have full-time jobs that yield them incomes that would greatly reduce their eligibility for most other types of student aid, but not for G.I. Bill benefits. Veterans using G.I. Bill funds are more likely than other students to attend low-tuition commuter institutions, since low tuition allows the veteran to allocate a larger proportion of the benefit to subsistence expenses.

Social Security Benefits

A fourth frequent source of aid as a matter of right is the social security program. A major purpose of the social security system is to provide dependents of deceased, aged, or disabled participants with income support to take the place of that which a former wage earner could have provided. Since a former wage earner would probably have tried to provide financial support for any children attending college, the Social Security Act was amended in 1965 to provide for continuation through college— through age 21—of the benefit payments payable on behalf of younger children. The amendment prevented a reduction in benefits when a student became 18. It did not authorize a separate benefit in addition to the benefits otherwise calculated as payable on behalf of the family. Moreover, because family size and limitations based on the former wage earner's earning history are also part of the calculations, the eligibility of a dependent for social security student benefits may result in a level of total family benefits little higher than if the student had been removed from the benefit rolls at age 18—in about a fifth of the cases, not at all higher (Congressional Budget Office, 1977, p. 6).

Because the social security student benefit is ambiguous in these ways, it has been difficult to assess its role in the student aid system or to take it into account in other aspects of the system. Clearly, families with a student member receiving social security benefits are better off as a group because of the benefit. Clearly also, they tend to be families with much reduced resources because the reason for their social security eligibility is loss of a wage earner. But it is impossible to say, except on a case-by-case analysis, whether student beneficiaries are needy or whether their social security benefits really reduce their need for other aid. This has been a problem for the various need-analysis systems. The Basic Grant program simply treats all social security benefits as parental income, subject to its usual procedures for estimating expected parental contributions. The CSS/ACT system partitions the nominal student benefit, treating part of it as parental income and part of it as student income in ratios varying with total family income from other sources.

The "Campus-Based" Federal Programs

The next programs the student aid officer relies on in building student aid packages are most usually the "campus-based" federal programs:

1. Supplemental Educational Opportunity Grants (SEOG)
2. Work-Study (W-S)
3. National Direct Student Loans (NDSL)

The SEOG program permits grants of up to $1,500 to students of "exceptional financial need"—presumably, those who have the hardest time in finding enough funds from other sources, either because their family resources are so limited or the costs of attending the institutions they choose are so high, or both. An SEOG grant may not exceed the sum of aid from certain other sources, with the intention that such a grant will not merely substitute for other aid available to the student.

The Work-Study program provides funds for part-time jobs during the academic year, and, if funds are sufficient, for summer jobs also. The jobs created are most often on campus and typically involve custodial work, research assistance, or clerical duties. Jobs may, however, be with nonprofit agencies and may include work in schools and hospitals. Work-Study funds pay up to 80 percent of wages, with the college or nonprofit agency usually paying the remainder.

The National Direct Student Loan program is the successor to the National Defense Student Loan program, the oldest general student aid program of the U.S. Office of Education. It provides loans of up to $5,000 over the period of a complete undergraduate program. The terms are very favorable: the borrower pays no interest while he or she is a student enrolled at least half-time, on military service, or in certain kinds of volunteer work. Even when the student's interest obligation begins, it is at a rate of 3 percent of outstanding principal.

These three programs obviously play different roles. The SEOG program provides additional grant funds to a relatively small number of students for whom the student aid officer believes they will be critical. The Work-Study program augments the number of jobs otherwise available to students. The NDSL program provides an alternative to other loan programs.

However, the similarities among the three programs are probably more important than the differences:

1. Each college makes an application for funds under all three programs at the same time and on the basis of a single set of projections of the need of its students for aid.
2. Funds allocated to the institution under any of the three programs are awarded by the student aid officer to meet need as estimated by the method chosen by the particular college among several acceptable to the U.S. Office of Education. It must be the same method for all three programs.
3. The method chosen constrains colleges in awarding their own aid funds in that they may not routinely add such funds to a package containing aid from any of the three programs if the student's total amount of aid would exceed by more than a modest margin the amount of need estimated using the chosen method.
4. The student aid officer has, however, great latitude in awarding aid from the three programs—in determining what the student's expenses are, how much parents can be expected

to contribute, and what burdens the student can be expected to carry in the form of jobs and loans.

Aid from Institutional Sources

Funds available to a student aid officer under these three federal programs can often be used almost as flexibly as the institution's own funds—sometimes more so. Accountability requirements are, of course, different, and the student aid officer can award the institution's funds, unlike these federal funds, without any determination of need, if the institution's own rules permit.

The sources of an institution's own aid funds bear discussion. They may come to the institution as gifts, the use of which is restricted to aiding students in general or to aiding special groups of students. They may be received as income from endowments subject to such restrictions. In the case of public institutions, the state legislature or a state board may provide funds similarly restricted to student aid purposes. A private college may, however, designate unrestricted funds for student aid through its own budget process. As pointed out in Section 3, a college may link its appropriation for student aid to its decision of how high to set tuition charges. At colleges where such decisions are linked, some part of the revenue from a tuition increase is often earmarked for additional student aid to students who cannot pay the increase or cannot be recruited if an offer of aid is not forthcoming.

Guaranteed Student Loans

The Guaranteed Student Loan (GSL) program is in many ways unlike any of the programs discussed up to this point and has a somewhat different role in the packaging of aid:

1. It is the least advantageous of the programs to the student. Accordingly, a Guaranteed Student Loan is often included in aid packages simply because discretionary funds under the aid officer's control are inadequate to meet need.
2. Students do not have an entitlement to Guaranteed Student Loans. They ordinarily can get such loans only if they can

find a willing private lender, usually a bank. But if they are successful, they are entitled to interest subsidies that increase with the amounts they borrow, and not according to their need. One interest subsidy amounts to 7 percent of their loan balances while they are attending college and for certain other periods. The other subsidy is for the life of the loan, but varies with interest rates generally prevailing in the economy. There is no longer an income test of eligibility for either subsidy.

3. The amount a student may borrow is not limited to need in the same sense that aid under the Basic Grant and campus-based programs is. The important difference is that the amount a student may borrow is not reduced by the amount of the expected financial contributions of the student and the student's parents. This means that Guaranteed Student Loans can serve as "loans of convenience," enabling families to spread their contributions over time, rather than make them all at once.

4. The funds lent are not public funds and do not appear on public budgets. Rather, the federal government or state governments (with federal insurance) guarantee loans against default. Accordingly, the costs that appear on public budgets are default claims, interest subsidies, and certain administrative costs.

5. Complex transactions are involved in originating a loan and redefining its status from time to time (for example, when it comes time for the borrower to begin making repayments). The student must make a separate application for a loan, distinct from any other applications for aid. The college, the lender, and state (or federal) officials must all scrutinize the application and make determinations of record concerning it on which the other parties must rely. If the loan is sold or pledged, still other parties become involved. If any party carries out its functions less than competently, confusion and disputes are likely to result.

Several problems have affected the usefulness of the Guaranteed Student Loan program:

- The program was never really designed as a vehicle for permitting loans to make their maximum contribution to meeting college costs. The statutory criteria for eligible loans have never permitted long enough or flexible enough repayment terms to enable students to manage the levels of indebtedness such terms could have made possible.
- Although a few lenders have sometimes found it attractive to make student loans, incentives for most lenders to participate in the program have generally not been strong enough to assure an ample flow of funds. Costs for origination and service have tended to rise more rapidly than yield, in part because of federal regulation of these activities. As a result, students have had a persistent problem in finding commercial lenders willing to make loans.
- The program has never had an adequate system of record keeping, and perhaps could not, given the complexity of the relationships described above. Record keeping problems have made it hard to keep track of borrowers and this, in turn, has been an important factor in high delinquency and default rates.

Food Stamps

Perhaps least amenable to the student aid packaging process are programs of assistance originally designed without the specific needs of students in mind. We can take as an example the federal food stamp program, although there are others, such as Aid to Families with Dependent Children. The participation of students in food stamps has varied widely from institution to institution—in one recent study of six institutions, from less than .5 percent to 13 percent of all students (*Food Stamp Act ...,* 1977, p. 116). A 1975-76 Carnegie survey of undergraduates found that 2.3 percent of students attending all types of institutions expected to receive food stamps, usually under $500 in value.

   If the institution is located in a county whose nonstudent population is relatively small, even a modest rate of participation among students can cause the proportion of all food stamp recipients who are students to be quite high. In one such county

where only 2.5 percent of students at the local university received food stamps, almost 30 percent of all households receiving them were student households (*Food Stamp Act* ... , 1977,
p. 117). Such cases have given the impression that students have
been massively taking advantage of a program that was not
originally envisioned as a student aid program at all. The Congress has taken several steps to reduce student participation
drastically by requiring students to meet increasingly complex
eligibility tests.

6

Recipients of Aid

Aid resources are concentrated on students whose family incomes are low—just the result we would expect of programs in which the amounts of aid that students receive are based on their measured financial need. As Table 10 indicates, students from families with incomes in excess of $20,000 received only a third as much aid per student from all sources in 1975-76 as students from families with less than $8,000 in income; yet the higher-income students attended college at roughly three times the rate of the lower-income students. The average amount of total aid and the average amount from each public program declines as parental income rises, except in the case of the federal student loan programs.

This exception tends, in fact, to prove the rule. A larger proportion of upper-middle- and upper-income students attend relatively expensive colleges. With their eligibility for grants limited by parental income, they are more likely to need to borrow. One would therefore expect average borrowings for these groups to be higher than for lower- and lower-middle-income groups.

Something similar can be said about the distribution of state grants and local or private grants. The average state grant does not decline as rapidly with higher income as does the average federal grant, and local or private grants even increase with income up to fairly high income levels. One would expect something like this to occur, although not necessarily to this extent. State grant programs have most often been enacted and funded

Table 10. Sources of undergraduate student support, by parental income, 1975-76

| | Percent receiving support from source | | | | | Mean amount of support[a] | | | | |
| | Parental income | | | | | Parental income | | | | |
Source	Total	Less than $8,000	$8,000-12,499	$12,500-19,999	$20,000 and over	Total	Less than $8,000	$8,000-12,499	$12,500-19,999	$20,000 and over
All sources						$3,251	$3,257	$3,117	$3,109	$3,512
Parental aid	61.2	39.8	59.5	66.5	79.1	1,085	433	722	991	1,833
Student self-support						1,108	1,083	1,041	1,138	1,056
Employment during the college year	43.3	39.1	44.3	46.5	44.1	516	611	499	504	451
Summer employment	42.3	28.7	44.1	50.8	49.2	292	158	275	359	351
Savings other than from summer employment	18.3	12.9	18.2	20.8	19.9	118	93	113	123	123
Spouse's earnings	9.7	11.2	8.8	8.1	7.3	182	221	154	152	141
Student aid						924	1,558	1,214	885	512
Basic Grant	15.7	40.6	26.8	11.3	3.1	132	404	197	71	27
SEOG	5.0	10.6	9.0	4.0	1.2	36	78	60	25	9
State grant	14.5	20.9	21.6	17.2	8.4	100	156	154	111	50
Local or private grant	9.6	8.3	12.3	12.0	8.9	79	61	99	93	83
Work-Study	9.9	16.5	14.7	10.4	4.7	64	102	96	64	33
GSL loan	7.7	8.9	9.7	9.7	5.7	108	107	125	144	90
NDSL loan	8.4	12.6	13.1	10.5	3.7	73	92	115	95	36

(continued on next page)

Table 10 (continued)

Source	Percent receiving support from source					Mean amount of support[a]				
	Total	Parental income				Total	Parental income			
		Less than $8,000	$8,000-12,499	$12,500-19,999	$20,000 and over		Less than $8,000	$8,000-12,499	$12,500-19,999	$20,000 and over
Other loan	3.7	3.8	4.4	4.9	3.1	$ 41	$ 34	$ 45	$ 51	$ 43
G.I. benefits	10.2	15.9	11.1	8.2	4.9	217	367	220	166	112
Social security benefits	6.2	14.5	8.5	5.1	2.2	74	157	103	65	29
Other support						134	183	140	95	101
Food stamps	2.3	3.7	2.6	1.8	1.4	17	27	19	9	12
Other public support	1.8	3.3	2.0	0.9	1.0	29	57	36	10	14
All other sources	7.4	8.2	7.5	7.4	6.6	88	99	85	76	75

[a]Means are calculated from data for all respondents, including those receiving no support from the source.

Note: In 1975-76, the Basic Grant program, with outlays of $905 million, was not playing as large a relative role in student aid as it did a few years later. Means were computed for all responding students so that amounts received from all sources would be additive and would indicate the relative importance of each source of support. The average Basic Grant awards received by student recipients, for example, were therefore considerably larger than amounts given, amounting to some $600 to $700 for those from families with incomes of less than $8,000—roughly the lowest income quartile in that year.

Source: Carnegie Council survey of undergraduates, 1975-76.

in order to help students afford private colleges. Local or private grants are most often awarded by such colleges from their own funds. Their relatively high tuition charges mean that some students who would not need aid at lower-cost colleges do need aid if they attend these institutions instead. Therefore, whatever system is used for estimating expected parental contributions, parental contributions will be exhausted by more students before they have met costs at high-tuition colleges. In a need-based system, we would expect to find that aid resources are concentrated where costs are high as well as where incomes are low.

The Recipients of Federal Aid

The percentages of students from families at different income levels receiving aid under the various federal programs are consistent with the average amounts of support received shown in Table 10 and the flow of aid funds shown in Figure 10. Figure 11 and Table 11 summarize the extent to which recipients are from lower- and lower-middle-income families.

Most heavily oriented toward low-income students (at least in the recent past) has been the federal Basic Grant program, with 65 percent of dependent recipients in the lowest family income quartile and 30 percent in the next lowest quartile in 1976-77. That is, 95 percent were from families with incomes below the median.[1] At the opposite extreme has been the Guaranteed Student Loan program, in which about 64 percent of the assisted students were from families with below-median income, and only about 25 percent were from the lowest quartile. Occupying intermediate positions, though with differing proportions of low-income students, were federal SEOG grants, Work-Study stipends, National Direct Student Loans, and SSIG grants.

State Aid

The award and recipient data summarized above do not disclose the considerable variation in the family income distribution of

[1]The proportion of recipients from families with incomes above the median will rise substantially under the impact of the Middle-Income Student Assistance Act of 1978, as discussed in Section 9.

Figure 10. Percentage of student aid funds flowing to dependent undergraduate recipients
from families with incomes below the median, selected programs, 1977-78

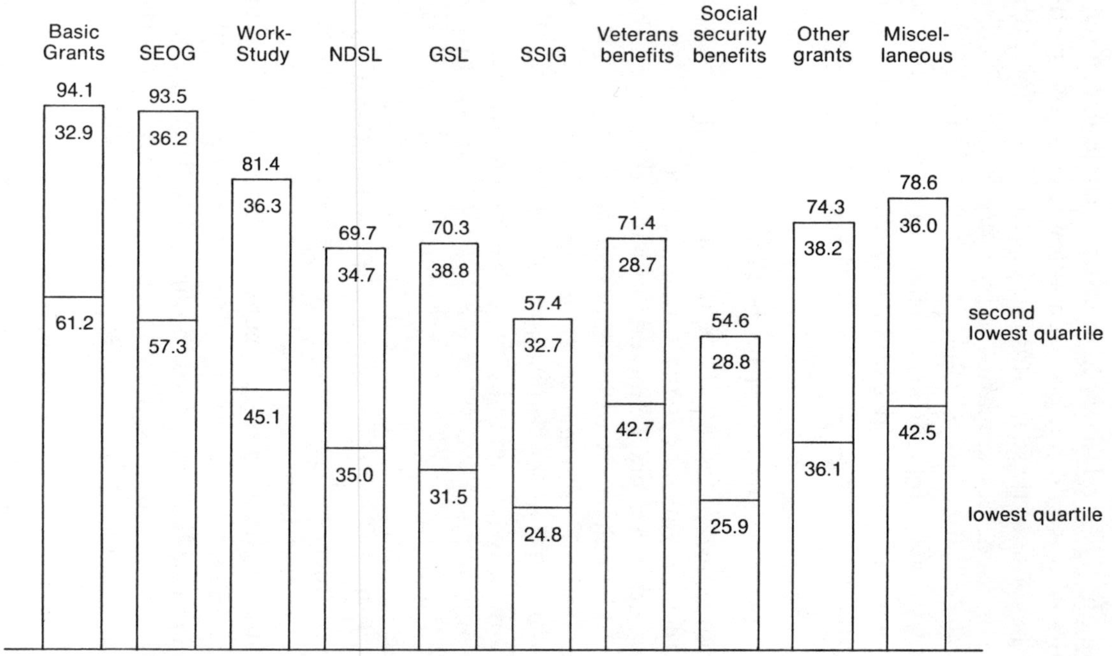

Source: Wagner (1977).

Figure 11. Percentage of dependent undergraduate recipients of student aid from families with incomes below the median, selected programs, 1976-77

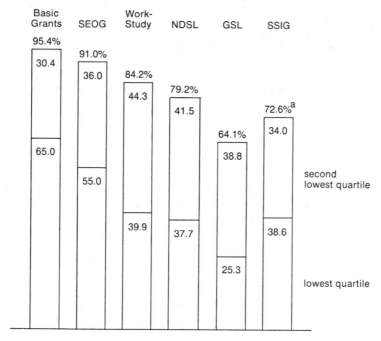

[a]Estimated from data for 1974-75 (Atelsek and Gomberg, 1975).

Source: For programs other than SSIG, computed from data in Atelsek and Gomberg (1977, p. 14).

state scholarships in different states. Most states use means test systems that are less restrictive than the schedule that has been used in the federal Basic Grant program. Many states have adopted the CSS/ACT schedule for at least one of their programs. Other states have their own schedules for one or more programs. Depending on the means test used, and differences in tuition costs from state to state, the income distribution of state grants can vary considerably. For example, the College Entrance Examination Board has found that in 12 states that account for a large proportion of state scholarship expenditures, 25 percent or more of student recipients were from families with incomes over $15,000, and in three sizable programs—

Table 11. Characteristics of students receiving aid under Office of Education assistance programs, 1976-77

Characteristics	Total[a]	Basic Grant	SEOG	Work-Study	NDSL program	GSL program
Number of recipients	1,937,000	1,411,000	432,000	698,000	751,000	695,000
	100.0%	100.0%	100.0%	100.0%	100.0%	100.0%
Sex						
Women	53.5	55.1	53.7	55.0	49.7	46.3
Men	46.5	44.9	46.3	45.0	50.3	53.7
Racial/ethnic group	100.0	100.0	100.0	100.0	100.0	100.0
Minority	34.9	43.0	39.1	29.3	25.7	17.0
Nonminority	65.1	57.0	60.9	70.7	74.3	83.0
Enrollment	100.0	100.0	100.0	100.0	100.0	100.0
Full-time	91.6	90.2	96.2	95.4	95.5	92.4
Part-time	8.4	9.8	3.8	4.6	4.5	7.6
Status	100.0	100.0	100.0	100.0	100.0	100.0
Dependent undergraduate	72.0	75.1	74.4	74.5	70.6	67.0
Independent undergraduate	24.0	24.9	25.6	20.5	21.6	18.4
Graduate student	4.0	—	—	5.0	7.8	14.6
Dependent undergraduates by family income quartile[b]	100.0	100.0	100.0	100.0	100.0	100.0
Lowest quartile	52.4	65.0	55.0	44.3	37.7	25.3
Second quartile	34.9	30.4	36.0	39.9	41.5	38.8
Third quartile	12.7	4.6	9.0	15.8	20.8	35.9
Highest quartile						

[a]Unduplicated count; excludes GSL program.

[b]Family income quartiles have been computed by the Carnegie Council from data relating to all families (U.S. Bureau of the Census, 1978b, Table B); families in the lowest quartile are those with incomes under $8,710, those in the second quartile have incomes from $8,710 to $14,960, those in the third quartile have incomes from $14,960 to $22,210, and those in the top quartile have incomes of $22,210 or more. It has been necessary to combine the third and fourth quartiles in this table because the highest income group for which data on student aid are presented in the source is $15,000 or more.

Source: Atelsek and Gomberg (1977, p. 14).

those of California, Michigan, and Minnesota—50 percent or more of the awards went to students from families in this income range (Table 12).

Table 12. Percentage of state scholarship recipients from families with incomes over $15,000, 1977-78

State	Percent
California	50
Colorado	45
Connecticut	25
Hawaii	25
Illinois	37
Maryland	35
Michigan	57
Minnesota	50
Missouri	28
New York	37
Pennsylvania	26
Vermont	36

Source: Hansen and Gladieux (1978, p. 7).

Income and Other Characteristics

Although the overall distribution of student aid favors students whose family incomes are low or whose costs of attendance are high, Tables 10 and 11 indicate tendencies in the distribution of aid which are, perhaps, surprising:

* Some students from relatively high-income families reported support from each aid program, even the Basic Grant and other student aid programs geared to low-income students. This is probably explained by the fact that they were from large families, had exceptional needs, or were from families with unusually high medical or other expenses.
* Members of minority groups account for a considerably larger proportion of federal student aid recipients than of all enrolled students because of the predominantly low-income status of minority group families. As might be expected, the

difference is most pronounced in the Basic Grant program, with its emphasis on low-income students. In 1976-77, 43 percent of the recipients of Basic Grants were members of minority groups, compared with 15 to 16 percent of all students. The difference is less pronounced in other federal programs, but nevertheless a disproportionate number of recipients are members of minority groups.

• Women are student aid recipients in relatively large numbers, accounting for more than half of the assisted students under federal programs, compared with about 47 percent of total enrollments in 1976-77. The probable reason for this is that among very low-income families the enrollment rates for women rose above those for men in that year.

• Although there has been some concern that college students have exploited the food stamp program, the data presented here indicate that the percentage of students receiving food stamps was very small and varied inversely with family income.

Independent Students

A growing category of students receive financial aid without regard to the incomes and other resources of their parents. These are the so-called "independent students" whose parents are determined to have no further financial obligation because of changes in family relationships. How independent status can be recognized where it is fair and appropriate to do so (and only in such cases) is a problem of considerable difficulty (Section 14). It is also a source of considerable anxiety among student aid officers and public officials because the numbers claiming independence have grown rapidly and because acquiring independent status is an important financial advantage for middle- and upper-income families. It means that no contribution from income and other family resources will be expected. Is this financial advantage an incentive that has led to the growth?

The growth has certainly been pronounced. The proportion of independent students among undergraduates receiving federal student aid rose from 18 percent in 1974-75 to 24 percent in 1976-77. In the Basic Grant program, 14 percent of the recipients were independent in the former year and 25 percent in the latter year (Atelsek and Gomberg, 1977). The proportion of students seeking aid who claim independence has risen even more rapidly. In the Basic Grant program this fraction increased from 20 percent in 1974-75 to 38 percent in 1977-78. Among applicants filing financial need data with the College Scholarship Service, it increased from 11 to 23 percent over the same three-year period.

There is no really good information on the incomes of the families of origin of these students. A claim of independent status is ordinarily an accepted reason for not providing parental income data on student aid forms. Many truly independent students simply do not know their parents' incomes. Those whose right to independent status is questionable may well not respond to questions about parental income in an entirely candid way.

Such evidence as is available does, however, suggest that independent students are more likely than other students to come from low-income families. One estimate is that, in 1976-77, 46 percent of full-time independent undergraduates, compared with 15 percent of full-time dependent undergraduates, were from families with incomes under $7,500, while a total of 70 percent of the independent versus 27 percent of the dependent students were from families with incomes below $12,000 (Froomkin, 1978, Table 2).

The College Entrance Examination Board has suggestive data for students who claim independence but who nonetheless supply parental income information—either through inadvertence or because of a policy of a particular institution to which they have applied for aid. The data for 1975-76 make possible the comparative percentage distribution of students shown in Table 13.

Further, the annual survey of entering freshmen conducted by the Cooperative Institutional Research Program shows that independent students are most likely to be found in institutions with large proportions of low-income students. The percentage of students who are independent is especially high in the black colleges. It is also relatively high in two-year and in public four-

Table 13. Percentage distribution of dependent and independent students
by income of family origin, 1975-1976

Parental income	Applying as dependent	Applying as independent
0 - $5,000	16.2%	28.2%
5,000 - 10,000	23.6	26.7
10,000 - 15,000	23.5	18.5
15,000 - 20,000	18.2	12.1
20,000 - 25,000	9.8	6.3
25,000 - 30,000	4.4	4.1
$30,000 plus	4.3	4.1

Source: Unpublished estimates of the College Entrance Examination Board.

year institutions. On the other hand, it is low in universities, especially private universities. These data tend to capture disproportionally the characteristics of those freshmen who enter college directly from high school, that is, those least likely to have established their independence from parental support. Even so, the freshmen data include a substantial proportion of independent students and indicate a decided inverse relationship between percentages of independent students and median parental income among types of institutions.

To the extent that independent students are found among older students—and the proportion of older students among undergraduates has been growing—they are usually employed and enrolled on a part-time basis and are comparatively unlikely to apply for student aid. The 1975-76 Council survey of undergraduates showed, for example, pronounced contrasts between sources of income for full-time and for part-time students, and part-time students were typically older than full-time students. Part-time students were relatively unlikely to receive any parental support and were considerably more likely than full-time students to be employed during college and to receive spouse's earnings. Part-time students were also quite unlikely to receive student aid, except for G.I. benefits.

Thus, the data we have located on the characteristics of independent students do not suggest that any substantial proportion of them is subverting the purpose of need-based student aid by seeking to establish independent status even though their parents are quite capable of contributing to their college expenses. No doubt there are such students, but they do not show up to any significant extent in the statistics.

This does not mean, however, that there is no independent student problem or that the problem may not become more serious in the future. In fact, the liberalization of income eligibility standards for independent students under the Basic Grant program, which was adopted by Congress under the provisions of the Middle-Income Student Assistance Act of 1978, will make it much more attractive for students to establish independent status. This is because much higher levels of the personal earnings of single independent students will be exempt from any contribution.

7

Impact of Student Aid
on Enrollments

Student aid programs have not operated in isolation. They have played a role in a larger context of educational and social change. Their influence on enrollments, in particular, has been in conjunction with that of other trends, other public policies, and changes in attitudes toward higher education.

The spread of low-cost public institutions, especially community colleges, has made higher education more accessible at the same time student aid has increased the numbers of young people who could afford it. From 1969 to 1975, large increases in the enrollment of veterans played an important role in sustaining enrollment totals, especially at public institutions. On the other hand, the reduction in draft calls after 1969 and the removal of the draft in 1973 have clearly been important in explaining a downward trend in enrollment rates for young males. Over this same recent period, a less favorable job market for college graduates has made a college degree seem somewhat less attractive than in times past, although this influence may have been more important in discouraging enrollment in the early 1970s, when an unfavorable job market for college graduates first appeared, than it was later on.

The Controversy over Enrollment Rates

It has been widely contended that rising college costs, and the resulting "squeeze" on middle-income families, have discouraged college attendance. In fact, in the last few years an extensive debate has centered on the behavior of enrollment rates by income groups, with some analysts using the data to show that enrollment of students from middle-income families declined until 1974, while others have emphasized the fact that enrollment rates of young people from middle-income families have revived significantly since then (Figure 12).

Much of this debate is inconclusive, and at least somewhat misleading, because there has often been a failure to disaggregate the data by race and sex. When this is done (Figures 13 and 14), it becomes clear that any decline in enrollment rates in middle-income groups until 1974 was entirely attributable to the decline in enrollment rates of white males. Furthermore, this decline, which has been arrested in recent years, affected all income groups in much the same manner. It clearly played a decisive role in preventing an overall rise in enrollment rates of young people.

On the other hand, if we consider enrollment rates of white women and blacks of both sexes, we find a very different trend. Among blacks, enrollment rates have risen for all income groups. The increases appear to have been most pronounced for blacks from the highest income quartile, although the small number of blacks from high-income families in the census samples makes the available data somewhat unreliable for this group. Enrollment rates of white women have also risen, but chiefly in the higher-income quartiles; enrollment rates of white women from families in the lowest income quartile have shown no tendency to rise. Strikingly, also, enrollment rates of black women exceeded those of white women for all family income quartiles in 1976, and by substantial margins. The same relationship held for black men (compared with white men), though not to the same extent, and not in the lowest income quartile.

The quartile boundaries referred to here were computed from data for all families—not for white and black families separately. This is appropriate if we want to compare enrollment rates of whites and blacks in similar economic situations. However, because the proportion of black families with low incomes is so much higher than the proportion of white families, the rise

Figure 12. Enrollment rates of primary family members aged 18 to 24 by family income quartile, 1970 to 1976

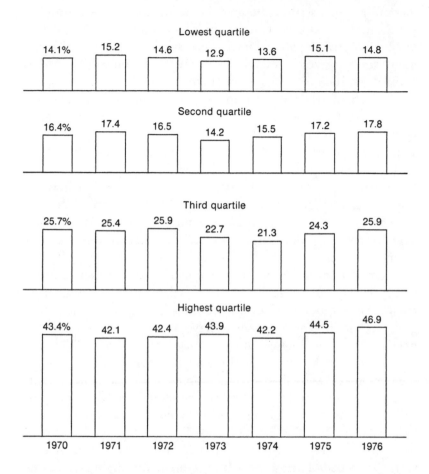

Lowest quartile

| 14.1% | 15.2 | 14.6 | 12.9 | 13.6 | 15.1 | 14.8 |

Second quartile

| 16.4% | 17.4 | 16.5 | 14.2 | 15.5 | 17.2 | 17.8 |

Third quartile

| 25.7% | 25.4 | 25.9 | 22.7 | 21.3 | 24.3 | 25.9 |

Highest quartile

| 43.4% | 42.1 | 42.4 | 43.9 | 42.2 | 44.5 | 46.9 |

| 1970 | 1971 | 1972 | 1973 | 1974 | 1975 | 1976 |

Source: Family income quartiles derived from income distribution of all families found in U.S. Bureau of Census, *Current Population Reports, Series P-60, Consumer Income,* money income of persons and families in the United States (annual, title varies). Numbers enrolled obtained from U.S. Bureau of Census, *Current Population Reports, Series P-20, Population Characteristics,* social and economic characteristics of students (also annual, title varies).

in enrollment rates of low-income blacks involved substantially larger relative numbers within the black population than did the increase in enrollment rates of higher-income blacks.

Figure 13. Enrollment rates of male primary family members aged 18 to 24 by race and family income quartile, 1970-1976

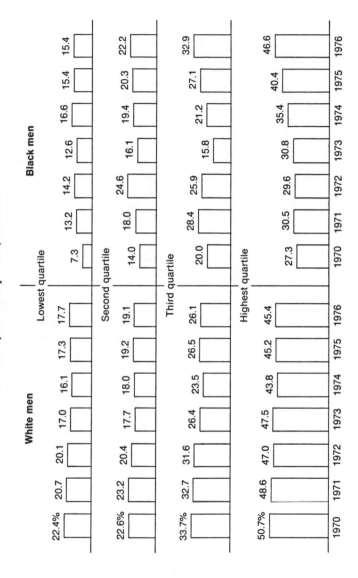

Source: See sources for Figure 12.

Figure 14. Enrollment rates of female primary family members aged 18 to 24 by race and family income quartile, 1970-1976

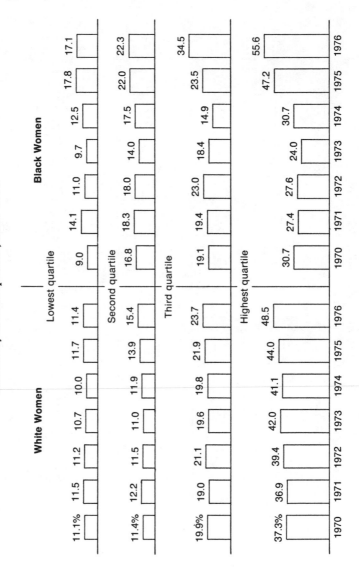

Source: See sources for Figure 12.

We have not attempted a similar income analysis for young persons of Spanish origin, because of limitations of the data. However, there has been something of a rising trend in enrollment rates for members of this group since 1972, when separate data on their enrollment first became available.

Why should enrollment rates of white men have behaved so differently from those of white women or of minority group members of both sexes? The view that the change in the draft was an important factor is supported by the uniqueness of the drop in enrollment rates of white men in the 1970s. It is also supported by the fact that a sharp rise in enrollment rates of white males occurred in the immediately preceding period, from 1964-65 to 1969, when draft calls were large. This suggests that enrollment rates had been inflated by a desire to qualify for draft deferment. It may well be, also, that white males were relatively more discouraged from enrolling than were other race and sex groups by the change for the worse in the job market for college graduates in the 1970s.

The relatively favorable job market for black college graduates that prevailed in the 1970s, well documented by Freeman (1976) and others, undoubtedly stimulated college enrollment of blacks. Black women evidently were especially motivated to take advantage of the changed opportunities.

Of interest, in fact, is the absence of any appreciable change in the enrollment rate of black men from low-income families after 1972, when the Basic Grant program was expanding. This is partly explained by the tendency of black men from low-income families to enlist in the armed forces. Between 1970 and 1977, the proportion of white men aged 18 to 24 who were in the armed forces fell from 16.3 to 6.7 percent. The sharpest decline occurred in the first few years of the 1970s when troops were being withdrawn from Vietnam, but the decline has continued quite steadily in more recent years. For black men, on the other hand, there was a decline from 13.6 to 10.7 percent from 1970 to 1973, but after that the percentage stabilized, so that by 1977 the percentage of black men in this age group in the armed forces (10.2) was appreciably higher than that for whites (6.7) (estimated from data in U.S. Bureau of the Census,

1978a). There is evidence, moreover, that black men in the armed forces are overwhelmingly from low-income families.[1]

These contrasting trends in the enrollment rates of white men and other race and sex groups have together affected the overall income distribution of college students. Census data on the family income distribution of college students, full-time and part-time, aged 18 to 24 show a slight rise in the percentage of students from families in the lowest income quartile from 1970 to 1976, a slight decline in the share of those from families in the next-to-top quartile, and practically no change for the other two groups (Figure 15). However, changes in income distribution differed from group to group (Figures 16 and 17). For white males, the changes somewhat resembled those for all students. Among white women, there was virtually no change in the income distribution of students. On the other hand, among blacks of both sexes—and especially among black women—there was decided narrowing of the income distribution, though with some reversal of the trend after 1974 or 1975. In the case of black men, this reversal may have reflected a decline in enrollments of Vietnam veterans.

Data on first-time, full-time freshmen tell a rather different story. They show an appreciable narrowing of the family income distribution of entering freshmen from 1967 to 1977 (Figure 18). The narrowing of the income distribution for women was more pronounced than for men. Most of the narrowing occurred, however, at least so far as the lowest quartile

---

[1]If we compare, for example, the number of primary family members aged 18 to 24 in the civilian noninstitutional population by sex, we find that the number of black men is markedly smaller than the number of black women in the lowest family income quartile, but that the difference is very slight in the three higher quartiles. Indeed, the data suggest that among black men from low-income families, the percentage in the armed forces is appreciably higher than the percentage in college. The apparent failure of the Basic Grant program to stimulate much increased enrollment of low-income black men is partly explained by the greater attraction of the volunteer army, with its comparatively high rates of pay.

Unfortunately, a reliable estimate of the number in the armed forces by income level cannot be developed from available data, because absence of low-income black men from the noninstitutional population can also be explained by institutionalization, including incarceration.

Figure 15. Distribution by family income quartile, primary family members aged 18 to 24 attending college, 1970 to 1976

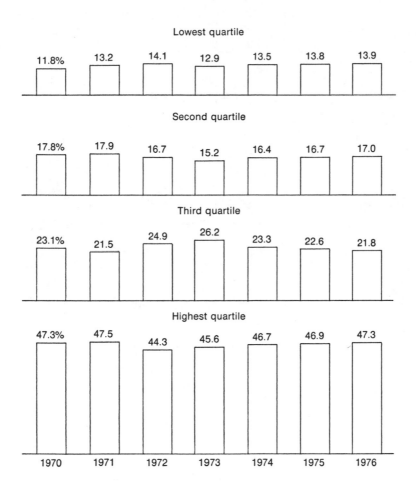

Lowest quartile

| 11.8% | 13.2 | 14.1 | 12.9 | 13.5 | 13.8 | 13.9 |

Second quartile

| 17.8% | 17.9 | 16.7 | 15.2 | 16.4 | 16.7 | 17.0 |

Third quartile

| 23.1% | 21.5 | 24.9 | 26.2 | 23.3 | 22.6 | 21.8 |

Highest quartile

| 47.3% | 47.5 | 44.3 | 45.6 | 46.7 | 46.9 | 47.3 |

| 1970 | 1971 | 1972 | 1973 | 1974 | 1975 | 1976 |

Source: See sources for Figure 12.

was concerned, from 1967 to 1972, and thus could not be attributed to the more recent expansion of student aid programs, and of the Basic Grant program in particular. The earlier narrowing is probably explained in large part by the growth of low-cost public institutions, by the three federal campus-based student aid programs, by social security student benefits, and

Figure 16. Distribution by family income quartile, male primary family members aged 18 to 24 attending college, by race, 1970 to 1976

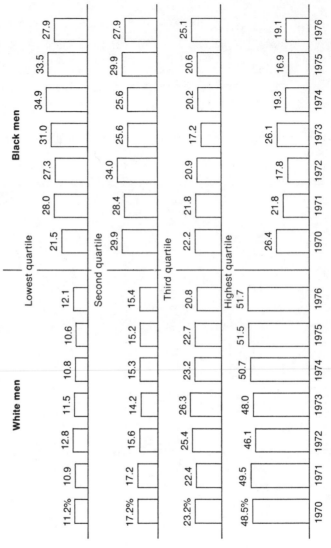

Source: See sources for Figure 12.

Figure 17. Distribution by family income quartile, female primary family members aged 18 to 24 attending college, by race, 1970 to 1976

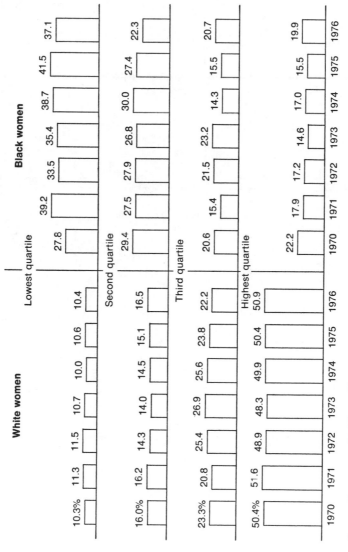

Source: See sources for Figure 12.

Figure 18. Distribution of first-time, full-time freshmen by family income quartile, 1967 to 1977

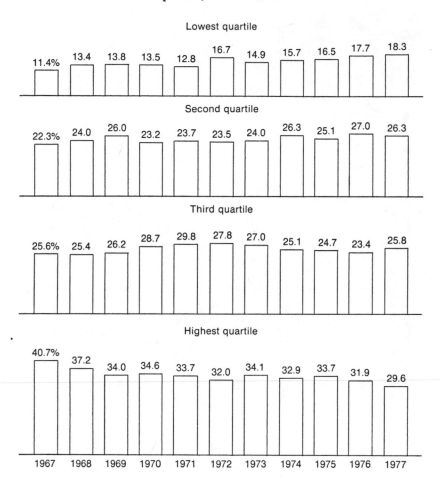

Lowest quartile

11.4% 13.4 13.8 13.5 12.8 16.7 14.9 15.7 16.5 17.7 18.3

Second quartile

22.3% 24.0 26.0 23.2 23.7 23.5 24.0 26.3 25.1 27.0 26.3

Third quartile

25.6% 25.4 26.2 28.7 29.8 27.8 27.0 25.1 24.7 23.4 25.8

Highest quartile

40.7% 37.2 34.0 34.6 33.7 32.0 34.1 32.9 33.7 31.9 29.6

1967 1968 1969 1970 1971 1972 1973 1974 1975 1976 1977

Source: American Council on Education (1967 to 1973) and Cooperative Institutional Research Program (1974 to 1978).

by the enrollment of veterans. This was also a period, of course, in which predominantly white institutions were making special efforts to open their doors to members of minority groups and to find ways of providing financial assistance to them.

Overall, the picture given by the freshmen data is one of a definite trend toward a more balanced distribution of enrollments by income as opposed to the lack of a clear trend in the aggregated census data. The explanation for this difference probably lies in part in the tendency for dropout rates of college students to vary inversely with family income. Thus, the freshmen data reflect the impact of student aid and other types of stimuli to the enrollment of low-income students, whereas the census data on all college students aged 18 to 24 reflect effects of the differential withdrawal rates for students of different income levels. To be sure, recent data also show that students receiving financial aid are considerably less likely to drop out than students not receiving aid (U.S. National Center for Education Statistics, 1978b, Table 3.14) but, even among those receiving aid, there is a strong inverse relationship with family income.

The Role of Student Aid

If we consider the evidence on who receives student aid discussed in the preceding section and the data on the changing distribution of enrollments in the present section, we are left with several conclusions. First, much that has been said in the debate over changes in the enrollment rates of students from middle-income families tends to be misleading. This is because, when trends are disaggregated by sex and race, we find that it is only among white males that there has been a decline in enrollment rates in the 1970s.

Second, the growth of student aid, along with such influences as the spread of low-cost public institutions, has narrowed income differences among first-time, full-time freshmen but not appreciably among college students in all college classes, although there has been a narrowing of the income distribution for black students. Third, differences in enrollment rates between whites and blacks have narrowed very substantially, especially if we control for income differences. Undoubtedly, the spread of low-cost public institutions, and particularly of open-door community colleges, has played an important role, but student aid must be playing a considerable role as well. That these influences, in fact, operate jointly is suggested by the particularly high percentage of minority group members among recipients of Basic Grant awards in public two-year colleges.

A further indication of the role of student aid, at least in maintaining enrollment, is the apparent decline in the proportion of students who drop out for financial reasons. Dropping out tends to carry a certain stigma and citing financial difficulties for doing so lessens that stigma. Accordingly, one cannot expect altogether candid responses from dropouts if they are given an opportunity to cite financial difficulties as a reason. Nonetheless, the trend of responses in studies that were at least somewhat comparable is suggestive. Respondents to Astin's survey of students from the high school class of 1968 gave financial reasons in 28 percent of the cases (Astin, 1975). The National Longitudinal Study of the class of 1972 received this response in 24 percent of the cases. A recent study of students from the high school class of 1975 conducted by the Higher Education Research Institute shows 8 percent.[2] Granting all the difficulties facing studies of dropouts, these figures indicate important relief from financial constraint on the educational careers of college students, and much of that relief has come from student aid programs.

[2]Unpublished data from the Higher Education Research Institute, Los Angeles.

8

Impact of Student Aid
on Institutions

Two views of the impact of student aid programs on different types of institution are widely held. First, the federal Basic Grant program is seen as having an important role in increasing enrollments at public community colleges. Second, it is widely understood that aid available to upper-middle- and upper-income students—especially state tuition grant programs and aid provided by the institutions themselves—has been critical to sustaining enrollments in the selective private colleges.

Both views are probably valid, but are hard to document fully. A third proposition, which can be documented, seems not to be widely recognized. It is that the federal Basic Grant program has played an important role in increasing enrollments of minority and lower-income students in the less selective private institutions.

The Flow of Aid and Student Choice

The distribution of federal aid recipients (Table 14) and the per student amounts of aid from federal and other sources (Tables 15 and 16) certainly confirm the view that public two-year college students have been relatively favored by the Basic Grant program. Tables 15 and 16 also confirm the view that students attending selective private institutions have especially benefited from state scholarship programs and aid from institutional sources (shown in the table as local and private grants).

Table 14. Distribution of total enrollment in higher education, compared with distribution of student aid recipients under major federal programs, by type and control of institutions, 1976-77

Type and control of institution	Total enroll- ment	Total recip- ients[a]	Basic Grants	SEOG	Work- Study	NDSL program	GSL program
Public	78.4%	72.6%	80.0%	63.2%	64.1%	61.3%	55.8%
Universities	18.8	19.3	16.6	17.7	17.8	25.8	25.4
Four-year colleges	25.5	24.8	26.9	24.9	25.5	25.9	22.4
Two-year colleges	34.1	28.5	36.5	20.6	20.8	9.6	8.0
Private	21.6	27.4	20.0	36.7	35.9	38.5	44.0
Universities	6.3	5.8	3.2	6.1	6.8	10.2	16.2
Four-year colleges	13.9	19.3	14.5	26.0	26.0	25.7	26.1
Two-year colleges	1.4	2.3	2.3	4.6	3.1	2.6	1.7

[a]Unduplicated count; excludes GSL program.

Note: Total of public and private students or recipients do not add to 100 because of rounding.

Source: Atelsek and Gomberg (1977, Tables 1 and 2).

These data show the tendency for aid to flow to those institutions students who are eligible for aid decide to attend. For example, a larger-than-average proportion of the students attending public community colleges are from lower-income families and are eligible for Basic Grants. This fact is reflected in the distribution of Basic Grant funds by type of institution. But this distribution of funds shows that the program favors lower-income students, not necessarily that it increases the tendency of such students to choose community colleges.

Annual freshmen survey data make it possible to trace, in some detail, the changes that have occurred in the income distribution of students in various types of institutions over a fairly long period (Table 17). They show that between 1967 and 1972, by far the largest increase in the percentage of students from the lowest family income quartile was in the public two-year colleges. But it was in the following period that funding for the Basic Grant program increased rapidly. And in this period, from 1973-74 to 1976-77, averaging data for the two pairs of adjacent years, increases in enrollment of lower-income students

Table 15. Sources of undergraduate student support in public institutions of higher education, by type of institution, 1975-76

	Research universities	Doctoral-granting universities	Comprehensive universities and colleges	Less selective liberal arts colleges[c]	Two-year colleges	Specialized institutions	All public institutions
				Mean amount of support[a]			
All sources	$3,395	$3,440	$2,942	$2,417	$2,698	$3,242	$2,963
Parental aid	1,518	1,277	883	466	394	910	823
Student self-support	1,089	1,216	1,142	1,166	1,238	1,216	1,181
Employment during college	397	492	506	601	723	588	577
Summer employment	417	379	320	215	162	268	275
Other savings	128	140	110	106	116	118	119
Spouse's earnings	147	205	206	244	237	242	210
Student aid	694	830	815	675	869	873	817
Basic Grants	60	95	123	139	138	117	116
SEOG grants	26	27	35	27	32	21	31
State grants	89	85	74	80	57	129	71
Local or private grants	62	50	37	31	25	52	38
Work-Study	54	65	59	71	54	54	57
GSL loans	111	123	91	58	54	96	82
NDSL loans	71	78	61	16	29	115	51
Other loans	27	53	42	11	27	47	34
G.I. benefits	113	156	212	165	388	211	261
Social security benefits	81	98	81	77	65	31	76
Other support[b]	94	117	102	110	197	243	142

[a]Means are calculated from data for all respondents, including those receiving no support from the source.

[b]Includes food stamps, other public support, and miscellaneous.

[c]There are very few selective public liberal arts colleges.

Source: Carnegie Council survey of undergraduates, 1975-76.

Table 16. Sources of undergraduate student support in private institutions of higher education, by type of institution, 1975-76

	Research universities	Doctoral-granting universities	Compre-hensive universities and colleges	Selective liberal arts colleges	Less selective liberal arts colleges	Two-year colleges	Specialized institutions	All private institutions
				Mean amount of support[a]				
All sources	$5,352	$4,232	$3,818	$4,704	$3,791	$3,155	$4,756	$4,167
Parental aid	2,872	1,884	1,581	2,688	1,484	1,422	2,157	1,903
Student self-support	907	1,300	889	653	813	619	1,052	885
Employment during college	308	612	348	158	306	184	299	327
Summer employment	423	435	331	307	297	234	436	344
Other savings	129	130	113	143	76	139	175	117
Spouse's earnings	42	123	97	45	134	62	142	97
Student aid	1,414	933	1,242	1,246	1,410	1,021	1,446	1,270
Basic Grants	92	99	224	115	253	286	88	184
SEOG grants	27	44	54	45	83	31	22	52
State grants	172	106	181	209	204	210	305	190
Local or private grants	431	144	170	260	188	91	153	207
Work-Study	78	64	69	121	124	77	67	89
GSL loans	256	154	201	193	136	82	357	189
NDSL loans	184	115	130	143	176	89	71	141
Other loans	74	48	63	68	62	37	124	65
G.I. benefits	45	99	90	16	100	39	158	82
Social security benefits	55	60	60	76	84	79	101	71
Other support[b]	159	115	106	117	84	93	101	109

aMeans are calculated from data for all respondents, including those receiving no support from the source.

bIncludes food stamps, other public support, and miscellaneous.

Source: Carnegie Council survey of undergraduates, 1975-76.

Table 17. Percentage of low-income students[a] among entering freshmen,
by type, control, and selectivity of institution, and sex, 1967, 1972,
1973-74, and 1976-77

Type, control, selectivity, and sex	*1967*	*1972*	*1973-74*[b]	*1976-77*[b]
Public universities	8.1	9.2	9.0	10.3
Men				
Low selectivity			7.9	10.2
Medium selectivity			10.0	8.5
High selectivity			6.8	7.6
Women				
Low selectivity			9.8	13.6
Medium selectivity			11.3	9.6
High selectivity			8.8	8.9
Private universities	6.1	7.6	7.2	9.8
Men				
Low selectivity			9.1	13.2
Medium selectivity			7.1	7.2
High selectivity			5.5	5.5
Women				
Low selectivity			11.0	14.9
Medium selectivity			8.5	8.5
High selectivity			6.0	6.0
Public four-year colleges	13.8	18.3	15.4	20.3
Low selectivity			18.7	26.8
Medium selectivity			11.0	12.2
High selectivity			12.6	12.2
Private nonsectarian four-year colleges	10.1	10.9	11.7	13.4
Low selectivity			14.2	19.4
Medium selectivity			11.1	12.2
High selectivity			7.6	9.3
Very high selectivity			6.5	6.2
Protestant four-year colleges	12.6	14.9	17.2	16.7
Low selectivity			28.6	30.0
Medium selectivity			11.7	12.8
High selectivity			7.9	7.7
Catholic four-year colleges	7.2	12.9	13.2	14.7
Low selectivity			17.1	20.0
Medium selectivity			10.8	12.1
High selectivity			10.1	11.4

(continued on next page)

Table 17 *(continued)*

Type, control, selectivity, and sex	1967	1972	1973-74[b]	1976-77[b]
Public two-year colleges	14.6	23.3	39.2	22.1
Private two-year colleges	14.3	18.6	20.1	23.4

[a]Percent in lowest family income quartile.

[b]Averages for fall 1973 and fall 1974, and for fall 1976 and fall 1977.

Sources: American Council on Education (1968) and Cooperative Institutional Research Project (1974, 1975, 1977, and 1978).

were not only slighter, but followed a somewhat different pattern. The largest increase in the proportion of low-income students took place in public four-year colleges. Moderate increases occurred in all other types of institutions, including community colleges, except for Protestant four-year colleges that had a large proportion of low-income students in both periods.

Thus, it is not true that growth of the Basic Grant program has been accompanied by a trend toward increasing concentration of low-income students in community colleges. Of course, the Basic Grant program has made it far more feasible for low-income students to enroll in community colleges, and the strength of this effect may be somewhat masked by the increasing attractiveness of community colleges to students from higher-income families.

Student Aid and the Selective Institutions

The role of student aid in sustaining the enrollments of the selective (and often very expensive) private colleges is surely important but hard to demonstrate precisely. For one thing, private college enrollments generally have become remarkably stable when the fluctuations due to increases and decreases in the enrollment of veterans are excluded (Figure 19). Given this stability, the positive effect of student aid for these institutions must largely have been to offset negative factors, most obviously the impact of high tuitions in a time of abundant places in lower-cost public institutions. The rapid growth of public stu-

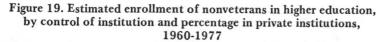

Figure 19. Estimated enrollment of nonveterans in higher education, by control of institution and percentage in private institutions, 1960-1977

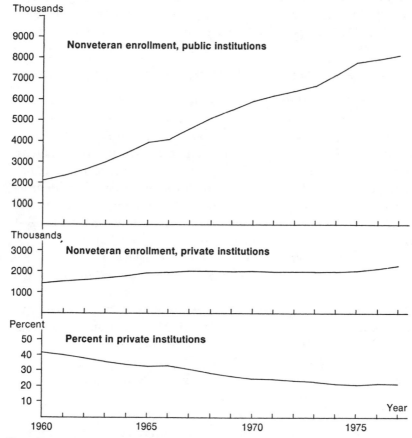

Note: Veteran enrollments deducted from total enrollments on the assumption that veterans were distributed between public and private institutions in the ratio of 80 to 20, the fairly stable ratio that has obtained in recent years.

Source: Computed by Carnegie Council staff from Office of Education and Veterans Administration data.

dent aid programs complemented the increased use of un-restricted institutional revenues for student aid purposes. The combination of public funds and their own efforts enabled the selective private institutions roughly to hold their own from 1973-74 to 1976-77 in recruiting freshmen from low-income families (Figure 20 and Table 17), while they also roughly maintained their total enrollments of students from higher-income families. All things considered, this was no small achievement.

Less Selective Private Institutions

However, the recruitment of low-income students by less selective private institutions seems to have been fostered in the recent period of rapid growth in student aid funds and, in particular, the Basic Grant program. The evidence seems conclusive that the increase in Basic Grant expenditures in recent years has assisted less selective private institutions in competing for low-income and black students. Of course, funds from other sources were often added to the aid packages of these students. But Basic Grants must have been critical to the total effort. In all of the groups of private universities and colleges shown in Table 18, the percentages of students receiving Basic Grants varied inversely with institutional selectivity. The percentages of freshmen receiving Basic Grants was even higher in the less selective private four-year colleges (Table 18) than in public two-year colleges (Table 19). An especially large percentage of students in the least selective Protestant colleges received Basic Grants. Many of these colleges are located in the South, and a number of them are private black colleges.

More important, however, is the fact that, apart from the consistently high proportion of low-income students in the Protestant four-year colleges, all groups of private institutions of low selectivity, as shown in Figure 20, made large gains in their proportions of low-income students in the period of rapid growth in the Basic Grant program. This occurred in a period when, as pointed out above, selective private institutions were losing ground in this respect about as often as they were gaining ground.

The case of the least selective private universities is especially interesting. The 10 universities in this category included

Figure 20. Changes in percentages of low-income students among entering freshmen in private institutions, by type and selectivity of institution, and sex, 1973-74 to 1976-77

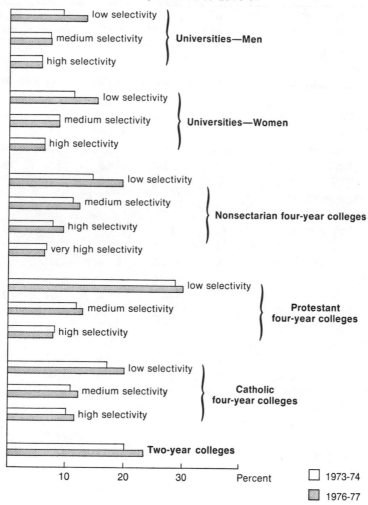

Source: Table 17.

in the weighted norms in the freshmen survey sample are almost all located in large cities. Nearly all of them lost enrollment between 1970 and 1975. In the following two years, some of

Table 18. Percentage of freshmen receiving selected types of
student aid, by type, control, and selectivity of institutions
and sex, 1977

Type, control, selectivity, and sex	Basic Grant	SEOG	Work-Study	State grant	College grant
Public universities					
Men					
Low selectivity	19.7	5.0	10.3	11.3	9.3
Medium selectivity	19.7	9.0	12.4	16.0	14.1
High selectivity	20.3	7.7	12.3	21.7	18.4
Women					
Low selectivity	22.5	6.5	11.9	13.1	9.5
Medium selectivity	22.2	10.2	14.8	18.9	13.1
High selectivity	19.1	7.3	13.3	21.5	17.5
Private universities					
Men					
Low selectivity	32.1	13.3	17.7	29.8	31.5
Medium selectivity	25.3	14.3	25.1	30.9	39.5
High selectivity	18.5	15.0	29.0	21.0	47.9
Women					
Low selectivity	33.7	12.9	19.2	31.1	31.3
Medium selectivity	21.1	14.1	28.2	31.0	42.6
High selectivity	17.7	12.3	30.1	19.9	43.2
Public four-year colleges					
Low selectivity	40.8	9.9	8.6	18.7	10.8
Medium selectivity	22.0	6.5	12.9	19.6	8.6
High selectivity	30.4	11.2	16.1	26.8	29.9
Private nonsectarian four-year colleges					
Low selectivity	42.7	15.4	24.8	19.7	24.3
Medium selectivity	32.5	13.5	27.2	31.3	42.0
High selectivity	24.5	9.7	29.7	32.1	45.6
Very high selectivity	17.7	7.4	24.2	22.5	39.8
Protestant colleges					
Low selectivity	55.9	19.9	34.7	32.4	30.0
Medium selectivity	38.0	13.6	29.5	36.5	45.4
High selectivity	29.3	13.1	30.3	34.6	47.9
Catholic colleges					
Low selectivity	41.0	21.3	36.8	32.7	30.6
Medium selectivity	34.7	14.9	30.5	41.4	43.4
High selectivity	33.5	14.6	24.9	42.9	42.5

Source: Computed from data in Cooperative Institutional Research Program (1978).

Table 19. Percentage of entering freshmen receiving support from selected sources and median amount of support, by type and control of institution, 1977

Item and type and control of institution	Parental aid	Basic Grant	SEOG	Work-Study	State grant	College grant	NDSL	GSL
Percent receiving								
All institutions	79.8%	32.7%	9.2%	15.9%	21.2%	16.8%	10.7%	13.1%
Public two-year	72.7	34.9	6.6	8.5	17.8	7.4	7.3	12.5
Private two-year	82.2	47.4	14.9	32.9	37.2	28.2	13.8	14.0
Public four-year	77.7	35.0	9.1	16.8	19.6	12.0	7.5	10.4
Private nonsectarian four-year	87.4	33.0	12.6	26.3	25.3	35.3	17.5	22.9
Private Protestant four-year	84.7	44.6	15.3	31.2	35.0	41.8	21.5	17.5
Private Catholic four-year	82.6	36.9	17.3	31.4	38.5	38.3	18.3	21.4
Public universities	87.0	20.7	7.4	12.3	15.9	12.6	9.8	9.3
Private universities	90.2	25.7	13.7	24.3	27.6	38.9	23.0	18.7
Public black colleges	65.6	79.9	28.1	31.9	18.2	11.5	14.4	10.0
Private black colleges	72.6	73.0	32.4	47.7	22.8	22.3	21.3	13.7
Median amount								
All institutions	1,020	740	less than 500	less than 500	less than 500	670	1,330	780
Public two-year	540	610	less than 500	less than 500	less than 500	less than 500	990	less than 500
Private two-year	1,160	930	540	less than 500	590	less than 500	1,320	900

(continued on next page)

Table 19 (*continued*)

Item and type and control of institution	Parental aid	Basic Grant	SEOG	Work-Study	State grant	College grant	NDSL	GSL
Public four-year	860	750	less than 500	less than 500	less than 500	less than 500	1,150	630
Private nonsectarian four-year	1,940	920	660	500	840	930	1,660	840
Private Protestant four-year	1,790	990	640	510	1,030	700	1,250	820
Private Catholic four-year	1,680	900	550	530	840	650	1,470	810
Public universities	1,640	740	less than 500	580	510	530	1,180	630
Private universities	3,180	1,010	820	720	960	1,490	1,490	880
Public black colleges	less than 500	910	560	less than 500	less than 500	580	890	less than 500
Private black colleges	650	1,290	610	580	770	900	1,200	530

Source: Adapted from data in Cooperative Institutional Research Program (1978, pp. 58-59).

them continued to lose enrollment, while others made slight gains; but there was a moderate loss for the group as a whole, and the annual average rate of loss was about the same as in the preceding five years. The increases in enrollments of lower-income students that accompanied the growth of the Basic Grant program may fairly be regarded as having been critical to the well-being of these institutions.

Changes in the percentages of blacks in the various types of institutions tend to reinforce these findings (Table 20). We should expect the pattern of changes to be similar because of the large percentage of black students who come from low-income families. And, just as the percentages of lower-income students tended to increase in the least selective institutions, so also did the percentage of blacks, and the changes were particularly pronounced in the least selective private universities.

Table 20. Percentage of black students among entering freshmen, by type, control, and selectivity of institution, and sex, 1967, 1972, 1973-74 and 1976-77

Type, control, selectivity, and sex	1967	1972	1973-74[a]	1976-77[a]
All institutions	4.3	8.7	7.6	8.6
Public universities	1.8	3.2	2.8	5.5
Men				
Low selectivity			2.6	6.1
Medium selectivity			1.1	2.9
High selectivity			2.9	3.0
Women				
Low selectivity			4.3	10.2
Medium selectivity			1.1	4.3
High selectivity			4.2	4.2
Private universities	2.1	4.8	5.0	9.9
Men				
Low selectivity			3.4	15.0
Medium selectivity			3.5	3.6
High selectivity			3.8	3.9

(continued on next page)

Table 20 *(continued)*

Type, control, selectivity, and sex	1967	1972	1973-74[a]	1976-77[a]
Women				
Low selectivity			5.8	19.6
Medium selectivity			5.7	5.1
High selectivity			8.0	7.4
Public four-year colleges	8.8	15.0	11.6	15.2
Low selectivity			17.1	22.7
Medium selectivity			4.1	4.9
High selectivity			7.3	5.8
Private nonsectarian four-year colleges	10.9	10.0	8.7	7.9
Low selectivity			11.2	13.4
Medium selectivity			6.5	4.3
High selectivity			3.4	4.2
Very high selectivity			6.2	4.2
Protestant four-year colleges	5.4	11.1	12.2	10.3
Low selectivity			26.3	27.0
Medium selectivity			3.9	3.9
High selectivity			3.8	2.6
Catholic four-year colleges	1.4	5.8	5.1	5.3
Low selectivity			8.8	10.7
Medium selectivity			2.6	1.9
High selectivity			2.5	2.2
Public two-year colleges	3.4	9.1	7.6	6.5
Private two-year colleges	1.8	4.8	6.6	9.2

[a]Averages for fall 1973 and fall 1974, and for fall 1976 and fall 1977.

Sources: American Council on Education (1968 and 1973) and Cooperative Institutional Research Program (1974, 1975, 1977, and 1978).

Although the Basic Grant program is generally regarded as a program providing access to the lowest cost institutions, it appears to have served—in conjunction with other aid programs —to have increased the feasibility of lower-income students choosing higher cost institutions. One can put a general conclusion this way: A program such as Basic Grants, which guarantees a "floor" of support, can affect enrollments positively at institutions costing far more to attend than the amount of the guarantee. It does so, presumably, by building a base of financial resources to which self-help, tuition grants, and other aid can be added, so the combined resources of eligible students are adequate across a greater range of institutional types. This generally positive view should perhaps be qualified in the case of institutions which credit a student's Basic Grant award toward tuition but do not make an adequate effort to assure that students can meet noninstructional costs appropriately.

9

The Changing Burden
of Financing
Higher Education

The long-run trend in the financing of American higher education has been toward the assumption of an increasing share of
costs by the general public, leaving a diminishing share to be
borne by parents and students. In 1929-30, families paid about
65 percent of the costs of higher education, while the taxpayers
shouldered about 22 percent of the burden and 13 percent was
met by philanthropic contributions. Over the years these proportions have shifted, and the change tended to accelerate in
the 1960s. By 1969-70, families were meeting about 39 percent
of the cost, the taxpayer 52 percent, and philanthropy 9 percent (Carnegie Commission on Higher Education, 1973, Tables
A-1 to A-13). This trend has continued in the 1970s. By
1975-76, the share of families was about 32 percent and that of
the taxpayer about 59 percent, while the philanthropic share
was holding steady at around 8 to 9 percent (Figure 21).[1]

---

[1]All of these estimates relate to shares of total monetary outlays on higher education, that is, educational costs of institutions plus subsistence costs of students. They
do not include three fourths of expenditures for research; nor do they include foregone earnings of students. Nor have we attempted to include in these estimates the
cost of public subsidization of loans under the NDSL and GSL programs. Although
these programs involve a public subsidy, they also involve increased expenses to students as they repay their loans with interest after graduation.

Figure 21. Changes in sources of financing higher education, selected years,
1929-30 to 1979-80

I. TOTAL MONEY OUTLAYS FOR HIGHER EDUCATION

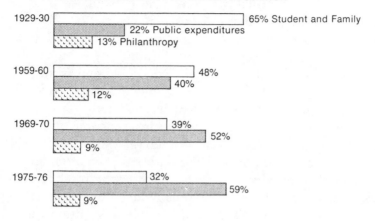

II. STUDENT AID EXPENDITURES (excluding veterans benefits)

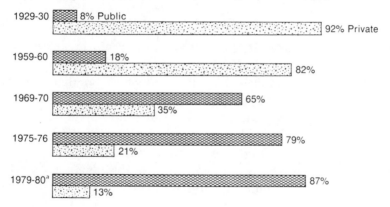

[a]Assuming expenditures of $2.6 billion for the Basic Grant program. Some of the components are estimated.

Sources: Carnegie Commission on Higher Education (1973, Appendix A); U.S. National Center for Education Statistics (1978a, Table 1); and Tables 6-10.

Until the late 1960s, the student aid portion of the public share of the costs of higher education was very small, except in the period of the post-World War II G.I. Bill. That part of the shift from private to public financing that occurred before the late 1960s mainly resulted from the expansion of public institutions and the subsidies that enable them to provide instruction at less than cost. An important fraction of these institutional subsidies benefited students whose families could not have afforded to pay the full costs of instruction. Over this period, therefore, the relative growth in the role of public financing cannot be regarded as resulting entirely from a shift in burdens to taxpayers from parents who could and would have paid more. Some could have, but many could not. The families who paid the much higher share of higher education financing in, say, 1929 were, on average, from higher-income strata than those who paid the lower share in the late 1960s. Nor did the share of financing paid by families with students attending the same type of institution decline as much as the total share for all families. The total family share is reduced by the increasing proportion of all students attending public institutions, which obviously had no effect on family shares for public or private institutions taken separately.

The Effects of Student Aid

In assessing the more recent role of student aid in shifting the financial burden still further in the direction of public financing, it is again essential to bear in mind which families received aid and what institutions their children attended. Until the mid 1970s, anyway, the bulk of student aid went to students from families from the two lowest income quartiles. Only a very small part of aid going to students from the lowest quartile could have represented a substitution of public financing for support that their families could have been expected to provide. Their families were relieved of burdens, to be sure, but they did not usually have the alternative of financing education through practicing routine economies in the way the notion of substitution would imply.

In fact, the question of substitution of public for private financing through student aid became a serious one only very recently. Partly for this reason, data relevant to the issue are inadequate. The issue was raised in the many discussions of the late 1960s and early 1970s concerning the tendency for the generous interest subsidies of the GSL program to give upper-middle-income families benefits they did not need. But three trends have made the problem a much more serious one now. First, the rapid growth of the Basic Grant program relieved other aid sources of some of the need to concentrate funds on the lowest income students, freeing funds for students from higher-income families. Second, state scholarship programs expanded also, in part to reduce the deterrent of high tuition that threatened the enrollment in private institutions of upper-middle- as well as lower-income students. Third, means tests have become less demanding, as documented in Section 4.

Public Policy and Public Financing

The recent impact of student aid programs on the long-run shift from private to public financing of higher education raises questions about the role it should play in distributing these financial burdens. There are no fully objective answers. There are, however, practical and political considerations that delimit the question somewhat. On the one hand, an excessive reliance on private resources would leave many families unable to provide enough support by practicing routinely feasible economies. Such reliance would not accomplish the public purpose of increasing equality of opportunity. On the other hand, a distribution of aid, however much, that made little or no distinction between the ability of families to pay, despite large differences in income that manifestly affect their ability to pay for things other than education, would be hard to defend in terms of the same equal opportunity goal. Aid distributed on such a basis would have to stand or fall on its merits as a kind of allowance simply for having children in college.

The Situation of Middle-Income Families

The recent national debate over the situation of middle-income students can be examined in these terms. It is, in effect, alleged that middle-income families are practically unable to find the resources expected of them. One type of evidence purports to show that, because of such financial constraint, enrollment rates of young people from middle-income families have declined.

But the evidence of enrollment rates tends to be misleading, for it is only among white males that enrollment rates have declined, and among them the effect is not confined to specific income brackets (see Section 7).

Another type of evidence much used in the debate involves a comparison of changes in college costs with changes in median family income over the last decade. The Congressional Budget Office (1978b, Table 2) showed that median family income for families with dependents aged 18 to 24 increased about 79 percent from 1967 to 1976, compared with a rise of 74 percent in student costs at public institutions of higher education and of 77 percent at private institutions. This finding, however, was disputed by a Library of Congress report (Esenwein and Karr, 1978) that pointed out that taxes paid by families at the median income level had increased by a larger percentage than income over the period and that after-tax income of median-income families had increased only 67 percent. The Library of Congress analysis showed a rise of 135 percent in taxes paid by median-income families, including the combined effect of increases in the federal income tax, the social security tax, and average state and local taxes. The increase in taxes is certainly a relevant consideration, although it should be borne in mind that the tax increases affect all middle-income families, with or without children in college. It is not obvious that higher taxes create a different and better claim for relief for families of college students.

In Figure 2 (Section 1) we have shown how changes in college costs have compared with changes in incomes of average upper-middle-income families and average lower- to lower-middle-income families. In the case of upper-middle-income families, incomes have tended to rise somewhat more than college costs, even after taxes, once allowance has been made for the less pronounced increase in expected parental contributions. The situation was similar for average lower- to lower-middle-income families.

Another point frequently made is that, because parents tended to have their children at rather close intervals in the 1950s, when most of today's college generation was born, it is more common for families to have several children in college at the same time than it was in previous decades. Indeed, the percentage of families with an 18-year-old child and at least one other child aged 18 to 21 rose from 34 percent in 1965 to 52 percent in 1978. However, family contribution schedules take account of family size and of whether or not a family has several children in college at the same time, and this must reduce the so-called "sibling squeeze" importantly. In any case, there will be a decline in the percentage of families with multiple children of college age from 1979 on (U.S. National Center for Education Statistics, 1978b, Table 5.14).

Certainly one point to be stressed is that aggregative statistics do not take account of the individual circumstances that make it difficult for some middle-income families to meet college costs. Means tests calculations may not take enough account of family size, age composition, and other factors and therefore may fail to moderate the variability of financial situations within family income brackets. And, obviously, families with children in high-cost private colleges face very different financial problems than families choosing low-cost colleges.

Financing Private Higher Education

Perhaps the most crucial factor is that many middle-income parents would like to see their children attend one of the prestigious private universities or colleges, where costs are now very high. Total costs of tuition, room, and board at Ivy League colleges tend to exceed $8,000 in 1978-79 (Suchar, Ivens, and Jacobson, 1978). Even though the range of incomes within which some student aid may be expected has widened very substantially, the family contribution at such institutions is likely to be large for middle-income families, especially if more than one child is enrolled. Some of the frustration of middle-income families probably stems from painful decisions for students to enroll in less costly institutions than those really desired.

Parents whose children attend high-cost private institutions tend to contribute a great deal more than those whose children attend lower-cost institutions, even though amounts of student aid awarded are large, on the average, at such institutions. And,

of course, the larger the income of the family, the less likely are
its children to receive student aid (at least in any form other
than loans). Froomkin (1978, Table 6) suggests that the average
actual parental contribution in 1976-77 for families in the
$15,000 to $25,000 income range was $930 for those whose
children attended low-cost institutions compared to $2,200 for
those whose children attended relatively high-cost institution.
Even more spectacular was the difference for families with incomes of $25,000 or more—from $1,620 in the case of low-cost
institutions to $3,800 in the case of comparatively high-cost
institutions. Froomkin's figures reflect the fact that parents of
children attending low-cost institutions benefit greatly from
public support of those institutions, whereas benefits derived
from public support are much smaller for parents whose children attend high-cost institutions, even though the value of public support in the form of income tax exemptions for dependent
students tends to be larger for such parents because of their
typically higher incomes (Froomkin, 1978, Table 7). An important factor in the pressure for aid or tax relief to middle-income
parents of college students must be a feeling on the part of
many middle-income parents with children in private colleges
that they are not receiving any of the benefits of the large institutional subsidies of public colleges and universities or much
benefit from those student aid programs that channel funds to
low-income students.

Tax Credits Versus Means Test Liberalization

If this account of the sources of lower-middle- and upper-middle-income pressure for tuition tax credits is approximately correct, then Congress was certainly wise to see the problem not in
tax terms but in terms of what might be wrong with student aid
means tests. Tuition tax credits are a heavy-handed and perhaps
self-defeating way of providing assistance to middle-income
families. This is the case for a number of reasons:

1. *The benefits they provide are not related to need.* Wealthy
   families would receive the same tax credit as less affluent
   families and, under proposals that do not provide for rebates

to families with very low tax liabilities, lower-income families would often receive no benefit at all. In some bills there
were also provisions for deducting any student assistance received before determining the tax credit, which would
reduce the eligibility of other lower-income parents for benefits. Under the bill approved by the Senate Finance Committee, 39 percent of the total benefits would have gone to
families with incomes of $25,000 and over, while under that
approved by the House Ways and Means Committee, 46 percent of the benefits would have gone to this upper-income
group (Figure 22).

**Figure 22. Comparative distribution by family income class, funds
flowing to students under Basic Grant program, before and after 1978
amendments, and to families under selected tuition tax credit bills
for college students, 1979**

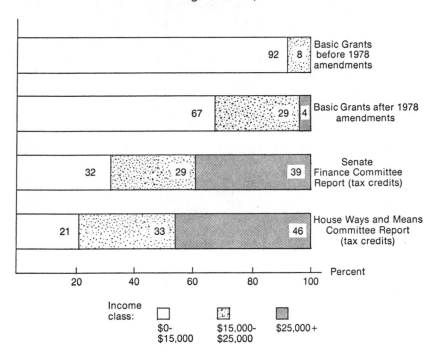

Source: Adapted by Carnegie Council from Congressional Budget Office (1978b, p.
xv).

2. *The benefits provided under tuition tax credit proposals are very small in relation to total educational charges per student, especially in the more costly private institutions, and yet would be very costly to the U.S. Treasury.* Under the House bill (H.R. 12050), the credit would have amounted to 25 percent of tuition up to a maximum of $100 in 1978, with the maximum rising to $150 in 1979 and to $250 in 1980. The estimated costs would have risen from $374 million in 1978-79 to $657 million in 1980-81.[2] The Senate bill (H.R. 3946) provided for a tax credit of 50 percent of tuition up to a maximum of $250 from 1978 to 1980 and $500 thereafter. The Congressional Budget Office (1978b, appendices) has estimated that the cost of postsecondary aid under the bill would rise from $751 million in 1978-79 to $3.9 billion in 1982-83, although these estimates did not take account of certain amendments adopted in August 1978, which would have reduced the costs somewhat.

3. *The temptation for colleges and universities to raise their tuition by the amount of the maximum tax credit would be very great.* Under existing provisions for student aid, colleges and universities are inhibited from raising tuition in response to increased public funding of student aid, because they must consider the impact of increased tuition on those upper-middle- and upper-income students who do not qualify for aid. But tuition tax credits would apply across the board to all families of college students, and thus the constraints against raising tuition by the amount of the credit would not be very great. To the extent that this would have been the response, the benefits would have flowed to institutions rather than to parents.[3]

4. *As contrasted with direct student aid, especially under provisions of state scholarship programs in many states, tuition*

---

[2]The bill provided for expiration of the credit after 1980-81, but this would have been an unlikely eventual outcome if the legislation had been enacted.

[3]It should be noted that under the House bill, families of students in low-cost public institutions would not have qualified for the maximum credit, which would only have been available (with a $250 maximum) if tuition were at least $1,000.

tax credits are not an effective way of aiding private institutions. Since the maximum tax credit is the same for all parents, it does not reduce the dollar tuition gap between public and private institutions. Moreover, because 80 percent of enrollment is in public institutions, the bulk of the assistance would go to parents of students in public higher education.

Redistribution of Burdens Within the Family

Changes in the officially expected levels of parental contribution are not the only factor at work in redistributing the burden of college financing.

A particularly interesting question, but one that is difficult to answer on the basis of available data, is whether student earnings have partially replaced parental contributions as a source of financing college costs. Or, to put the question somewhat differently, if the family share in the burden of financing has been declining, has the parental share declined even more because student earnings are becoming a rising proportion of the total family contribution? A careful review of studies of sources of student support—dating from about 1962 to 1976—suggests some tendency for the relative role of student earnings to rise and of parental support to fall[4] even after allowing for the impact of increased relative enrollment in low-cost public institutions. This conclusion, however, is somewhat tentative because the available studies are not comparable in terms of the types of students included or in terms of sources of support specifically investigated.

Some additional light on changes in sources of student support from 1969 to 1975-76 is shed by the data in Table 21. There was a substantial decline in the percentage of students reporting parental support, but the decline was particularly pronounced for those from the lowest family income quartile and became steadily less marked with increasing family income.

---

[4]The only study that seems inconsistent with this finding is that based on the 1976 Survey of Income and Education, data from which were analyzed by Froomkin (1978). However, that study did not include independent students, whereas such students were apparently included in most other studies.

Table 21. Percentage of undergraduates receiving some support from selected sources, by family income quartile, 1969 and 1975-76 (includes only nonveterans)

Source	Total 1969	Total 1975-76	Lower quartile 1969	Lower quartile 1975-76	2nd quartile 1969	2nd quartile 1975-76	3rd quartile 1969	3rd quartile 1975-76	Top quartile 1969	Top quartile 1975-76
Family support	82.6%	67.5%	69.7%	46.7%	78.2%	65.4%	87.1%	71.8%	90.8%	82.2%
Savings from summer employment[b]	53.3	46.2	60.5	33.1	58.0	48.0	51.1	54.5	45.4	50.9
College year employment	n.a.	42.7	n.a.	37.5	n.a.	43.5	n.a.	45.5	n.a.	43.5
Work-study grant	9.0	10.7	n.a.	19.4	n.a.	16.2	n.a.	11.0	n.a.	4.8
Spouse's employment	9.0	8.8	12.9	9.9	9.4	7.9	6.5	7.4	6.5	6.3
Scholarships	39.8	n.a.	55.4	n.a.	47.0	n.a.	38.0	n.a.	25.6	n.a.
BEOG		16.9		48.2		28.8		12.1		3.1
SEOG		5.4		12.5		9.8		4.3		1.3
State grant		15.4		24.0		23.0		18.1		8.5
Local or private grant		10.5		9.9		13.5		12.8		9.2
Loan	26.9	n.a.	41.7	n.a.	32.8	n.a.	24.3	n.a.	13.2	n.a.
Federal guaranteed loan		8.2		10.2		10.3		10.2		5.7
National Direct Student Loan		9.0		14.8		14.2		11.0		3.7
Other loan		3.9		4.1		4.6		5.2		3.2
Other savings[b]		19.3		13.8		19.1		21.6		20.0
Other	16.5	n.a.	24.1	n.a.	17.1	n.a.	14.8	n.a.	13.5	n.a.
Social Security benefits		6.8		17.5		9.4		5.6		6.6
Other		7.2[a]		8.4[a]		7.2[a]		7.2[a]		6.4[a]

[a]Does not reflect small percentage receiving food stamps and other public support (see Table 7).

[b]Data on these items for 1969 are omitted, because they are not considered comparable with data for 1975-76.

Sources: Carnegie Commission survey of undergraduates, 1969; and Carnegie Council survey of undergraduates, 1975-76.

Unfortunately, the data relating to earnings are more difficult to interpret, because no separate question was asked about Work-Study earnings in 1969, and it appears that the combined percentages of those reporting Work-Study earnings and term-time employment in 1975-76 roughly equal or exceed the percentages reporting termtime employment in 1969 in most income groups. There appeared to have been a sharp drop in proportions reporting savings from summer employment and other savings, but we have not shown the 1969 data on these items in the table because of doubts about their comparability with data from the later survey. We have excluded veterans from the data, because the large increase in enrollment of veterans between the two years could have markedly affected the comparisons.

The data on scholarships and loans are also somewhat difficult to interpret, because some students responding to the more detailed questions asked in 1975-76 probably received scholarships from more than one source, and some may have received loans from more than one source.

Nevertheless, the data strongly suggest that patterns of support changed substantially between the two surveys, primarily for those from relatively low-income families, with scholarships to some degree replacing other sources of support. In interpreting the data, however, two factors should be kept in mind. In 1975-76, there were more minority group families with children in college than there had been in 1969, and this could well mean that, within the lowest family income quartile, there had been a shift to families with especially low incomes. Another complication is that 1969 was a year characterized by full employment, when job opportunities for college students were very favorable, whereas 1975-76 was a year of substantial unemployment. This could well help to explain the sharp drop in the percentage reporting summer employment between the two years.

Although it is not possible to draw very exact conclusions about changes in the relative amounts of parental support because of differences in the way the questions were asked, we have developed some rough estimates that indicate that parents were contributing about 20 percent fewer dollars in 1975-76 than they would have been if they had continued to contribute at the same rate as in 1969 (allowing for the increase in enrollment and the rise in college costs). Again, however, the important point is that the reduction was considerably greater for parents in the lowest family income quartile and declined steadily with advancing family income. When estimated parental savings are compared with the increase in student aid over the period, parental savings appear to represent perhaps one half to two thirds of the increased dollars flowing into student aid, but these benefits, in relative terms, accrued primarily to low-income families.

Part Three

Opportunities for Improvement

10

Clarifying the Role of Student Earnings

Employment has always been a major resource for students whose parents could not meet their college expenses. Indeed, having worked one's way through college has been regarded as a special distinction. Those who have done so often seem to have had (or acquired) a special ability to concentrate their efforts on a goal and this ability has served them well throughout their subsequent careers. This view of student self-support is the basis for the great popularity and firm political support of the College Work-Study program. Data on recent undergraduates who are employed tends to confirm the positive appraisal of work. Students who work part-time are usually less likely to drop out (Astin, 1975, Chapter 4).

The character of student jobs has changed in the last two decades, and in desirable directions. Traditionally, the student who worked his way through college had few other resources and had little if anything to fall back on if earnings failed to cover expenses. It might be necessary to drop out for a time to accumulate savings and then to reenroll. The restricted employment opportunities open to women made working one's way even harder for them than for men. Some students undoubtedly worked longer hours than was consistent with the academic achievement of which they were capable.

The growth in student grants and loans has greatly reduced these negative aspects of reliance on earnings. On the one hand, student aid officers are in a position to provide grants to reduce employment burdens that would exceed the maximum commitment of the student's time that would be desirable in terms of the student's academic load. On the other hand, by using Work-Study funds, the student aid officer often can provide jobs to students who cannot otherwise find them. Whether or not the student aid officer intervenes in either of these ways, earnings are generally regarded as a resource to be considered in the student aid packaging process. This means that the student aid officer is in a position to monitor the situations of individual students and to exert a strong influence in the direction of devoting reasonable and desirable amounts of time to jobs.

The institutional context of this role of the student aid officer may, however, differ considerably:

- Institutional allocations of Work-Study funds have not adequately reflected the relative difficulty students encounter in finding nonsubsidized employment in the communities where the institutions are located. Accordingly, some institutions have received more Work-Study funds than they could spend in creating serious jobs, others far less.[1]
- The institution may have a policy of creating or reserving campus jobs for students, with wages paid out of regular operating funds. The student aid officer may have a role in filling these jobs, in referring students to them or simply in adjusting the amount of students' need to reflect the amount of their earnings in such jobs.
- The institution may have a policy of expecting all students who apply for aid to find jobs that will provide them with specified amounts of earnings. Such jobs may be on- or off-campus and found through a student employment office or by individual job search.
- The institution may have a program of cooperative education

---

[1]Institutions have returned substantial amounts of Work-Study funds they could not use to the U.S. Office of Education. These funds are reallocated to other institutions. In fiscal year 1976 the amount returned was $50 million; in 1977, $28 million; and in 1978 $23 million.

in which all students take full-time jobs coordinated with the academic calendar. The student aid office will take earnings from such jobs into account.

Influences other than that of the student aid system have also been generally benign. There has been enormous growth in those economic sectors that can readily accept part-time workers. Attitudes of students have also changed: it is accepted as a matter of course that fellow students work and loss of status rarely results from having to work. Restrictions on the availability of jobs to women students have been reduced.

Data on Student Earnings

For all of these reasons, students are probably working more and earning more similar amounts than ever before. Figure 23 shows the growth in labor force participation by students aged 18 to 24. The 1975-76 Carnegie Council survey of undergraduates (Tables 22 and 23) indicates that the average combined summer and termtime earnings available to meet college amounted to $808. White men had on average about $250 more in such earnings and black women about $300 less, with white women and black men earning intermediate amounts. The average combined earnings of students distinguished only by parental income differed by small amounts—less than $100 from the lowest to the highest income groups. But the differences tended to be larger for black students (both men and women) across differing parental incomes and the share of total available earnings coming from summer employment was much higher for white men than for white women or for blacks of either sex.

These differences no doubt result importantly from differences in ability to find jobs, reflected in the much lower percentages of students with available earnings among minority groups, especially from summer jobs. There also may be differences among income groups in the extent to which summer earnings go into the family budget and therefore become unavailable for meeting college expenses.

Earnings are regarded as a major source of support among students attending all kinds of institutions. There are, however,

Figure 23. Percentage of students aged 18 to 19 and 20 to 24 in the
labor force, by sex, 1947 to 1976

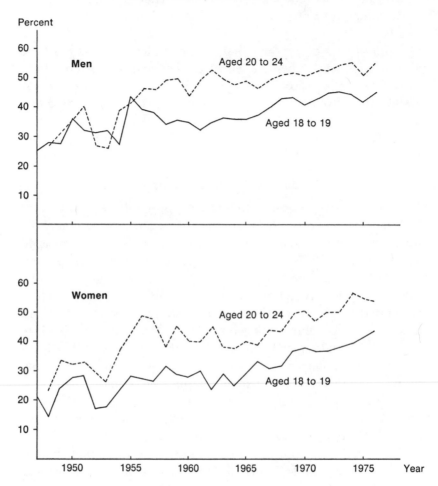

Source: President of the United States (1978).

differences among types of institutions in the relative amounts
of expense students expect to cover from summer as against
termtime employment. On the one hand, students attending
highly selective institutions count more on summer than on
termtime earnings. The reverse is true of less selective institutions (Tables 15 and 16). In public community colleges there

Table 22. Percentage of undergraduates with earnings from employment during termtime and mean amounts earned, by parental income, race or ethnic group, and sex, 1975-76

Race or ethnic group and sex	Percentage with income from employment in termtime by parental income					Mean for all respondents by parental income					Mean for those with earnings by parental income				
	Total	Under $8,000	$8,000 to 12,499	$12,500 to 19,999	$20,000 and over	Total	Under $8,000	$8,000 to 12,499	$12,500 to 19,999	$20,000 and over	Total	Under $8,000	$8,000 to 12,499	$12,500 to 19,999	$20,000 and over
Total	43.3	39.1	44.3	46.5	44.1	$516	$611	$499	$504	$451	$1,193	$1,562	$1,128	$1,082	$1,024
Men	46.7	43.2	46.3	50.8	47.4	646	751	598	636	581	1,381	1,741	1,293	1,252	1,225
Women	39.8	34.9	42.0	41.4	40.8	384	461	394	338	328	965	1,319	938	815	803
White	45.0	45.5	45.9	47.2	44.3	525	711	501	506	452	1,166	1,564	1,091	1,072	1,021
Men	48.3	47.5	47.2	51.5	47.8	660	837	608	645	581	1,366	1,762	1,288	1,254	1,215
Women	41.7	43.2	44.4	42.0	41.0	384	560	383	329	329	921	1,297	863	783	802
Black	29.0	26.2	31.9	32.8	34.9	447	376	554	335	531	1,540	1,437	1,737	1,020	1,522
Men	32.6	29.4	37.5	39.2	34.6	522	403	648	396	935	1,603	1,369	1,727	1,009	2,704[b]
Women	26.5	23.4	27.4	25.9	35.6	393	358	479	270	308	1,483	1,529	1,748	1,040	865
Other minority[a]	38.6	29.5	41.6	47.1	42.6	500	488	454	612	392	1,293	1,654	1,091	1,298	919
Men	42.6	38.0	46.8	50.0	43.9	579	682	502	633	452	1,358	1,794	1,072	1,267	1,030
Women	33.4	19.3	35.1	43.8	39.9	398	253	395	564	336	1,189	1,313	1,124	1,288	841

[a]Includes Native Americans, Mexican Americans, Puerto Ricans, other Latin Americans, Orientals, other Asians, and all others.

[b]Mean unreliable because of small number of sample cases.

Source: Carnegie Council survey of undergraduates, 1975-76.

Table 23. Percentage of undergraduates with earnings from summer employment and mean amounts earned, by parental income, race or ethnic groups, and sex, 1975-76

Race or ethnic group and sex	Percent with income from summer employment, by parental income					Mean for all respondents, by parental income					Mean for those with earnings, by parental income				
	Total	Under $8,000	$8,000 to 12,499	$12,500 to 19,999	$20,000 and over	Total	Under $8,000	$8,000 to 12,499	$12,500 to 19,999	$20,000 and over	Total	Under $8,000	$8,000 to 12,499	$12,500 to 19,999	$20,000 and over
Total	42.3	28.7	44.1	50.8	49.2	$292	$158	$275	$359	$351	$691	$552	$623	$706	$713
Men	43.8	29.8	45.5	51.5	51.0	361	194	333	435	433	825	650	733	843	849
Women	40.9	27.7	42.8	49.9	47.5	222	123	216	266	273	544	445	505	533	574
White	44.8	31.9	46.8	51.9	49.6	313	182	299	369	358	699	571	638	711	722
Men	45.9	31.2	48.1	52.6	51.2	386	221	365	445	442	841	710	759	846	864
Women	43.9	32.9	45.8	51.0	48.4	239	139	232	276	278	545	423	507	542	575
Black	25.0	23.8	29.7	31.5	37.9	130	111	171	137	156	520	466	577	434	411
Men	26.5	26.2	29.4	27.8	44.8	147	91	176	157	167	555	349	600	566	372[b]
Women	24.0	21.7	30.0	36.0	33.0	119	124	167	115	148	495	570	559	320	449
Other minority[a]	30.9	21.8	32.5	46.7	43.7	191	125	159	275	254	617	576	490	588	582
Men	35.6	28.8	35.2	51.2	50.2	245	186	189	344	307	688	647	535	671	611
Women	25.2	14.4	29.1	41.7	36.5	127	61	122	201	203	505	421	421	481	555

[a]Includes Native Americans, Mexican Americans, Puerto Ricans, other Latin Americans, Orientals, other Asians, and all other.

[b]Mean unreliable because of small number of sample cases.

Source: Carnegie Council survey of undergraduates, 1975-76.

appears to be an especially strong pay-as-you-go attitude. Students at these institutions expect the bulk of budgeted earnings to come from termtime employment. The rates of termtime employment can be very high in these institutions, in part because so many of their students are part-time. In the Los Angeles Community College system, for example, almost three quarters of the students attending have jobs and about a third have jobs that are full-time or nearly so.[2]

How Much Can Students Be Expected to Earn?

Data on students in 1975-76 who did have money from either summer or termtime employment gives some idea of how much students can usually contribute from earnings if they can find jobs both in the summer and at termtime. An average student who had a summer job and also received average termtime earnings of students who had jobs would have had, after meeting their expenses during the summer, over $1,800 available for college expenses from the two sources together. The corresponding amount for black women—the most disadvantaged group when average earnings for an entire group (with and without jobs) were examined—would be even more, over $1,900. The least such combined amount was $1325 for middle-income white women. If student earnings have been rising at least at the rate of increases in the federal minimum wage, the amount that can now typically be earned toward college expenses by this lowest earning group—middle-income white women—is $1670 if they can find both summer and termtime jobs.

Financial aid officers ordinarily expect students to provide for less than this amount toward college expenses. Many students who now have both summer and termtime jobs are either relieving their parents of part of their expected financial contributions or are enjoying a somewhat higher standard of living than their student aid packages alone would allow.

The amount of expected earnings assumed as part of the student's resources to which aid will be added in the packaging process is, if anything, even less consistent from college to college than it was a few years ago. There are several reasons:

[2]Information provided by the Los Angeles Community College District.

- Differing earnings opportunities for a typical student are assumed by different colleges.
- Some colleges have quite demanding self-help expectations but then substitute loans or other aid funds if it proves difficult for students to earn as much as expected.
- Traditionally, most colleges have assumed a contribution from summer employment equal to net earnings after meeting subsistence costs during the summer months. However, some colleges, faced with the increased need for aid among their students when calculated by the newer CSS/ACT standards, have recaptured some of the lost direct parental contributions by assuming that parents will meet subsistence costs during the summer months and not deducting these costs from expected gross summer earnings. The additional amount the parents are expected to provide the student during the summer months increases the amount the student can be expected to provide from summer savings toward termtime expenses.

A consensus on the role of student earnings and loans in financing college expenses would help to avoid the unfairness that may result from these wide differences among institutional policies. This would require establishing a standard student earnings expectation. Council Recommendations 1 through 7 in Section 2 suggest workable ground rules for a standard meeting these conditions.

11

Strengthening the Need-Based System

For the next decade, at least, parents will have to continue to bear very substantial burdens in financing the higher education of their offspring. For the public to assume the entire burden parents have traditionally borne would cost at least $10 billion in additional public expenditures. There is no reason to think that additional expenditures in this amount have the priority, urgency, and popular support such a policy would call for.

Nor can self-help on the part of students themselves be expected to grow in the near future to the extent necessary to relieve parents of their remaining financial burdens. The feasible level of a student earnings expectation will rise, but only gradually with increases in productivity, wages, and the continued spread of labor market arrangements favorable to part-time employment. Manageable levels of self-help in the form of borrowing will also rise only gradually, since loans must be repaid out of only gradually improving incomes later in life.

If parents in general must continue to finance a sizeable share of the educational expenses of their children, there is no good alternative to distributing student aid grants and equivalent subsidies inversely according to ability to pay. This means assessing costs of attendance and available family resources, calculating need as the difference and awarding aid to cover the gap between the two.

No one seriously proposes completely doing away with these elements of a need-based system. Tax credits or grants invariant with income are proposed, but it usually seems to be assumed that a need-based aid system would continue alongside such aid. But a number of developments have tended in the direction of reduced emphasis on need in the calculation of aid awards:

- Relaxed means tests, such that fewer and fewer families are expected to pay full costs
- Proposals for general tax relief of families with college students
- Elimination of income tests of eligibility for student loan interest subsidies
- Criteria for establishing independent student status, under which children of upper-middle- and upper-income families can sometimes qualify for as much aid as children of lower-income parents

So far, it has been at least arguable that the trend toward less emphasis on differences in family resources in the awarding of aid has not been at the expense of students from lower-income families. On the surface, at least, it appears that the increased eligibility of middle- and upper-income students for aid has been on top of the recognized eligibility of lower-income students for assistance. It is difficult to argue against this view, because no one can really know whether more aid would have been made available to lower-income students if the claims of less needy students had not been recognized. But it is hard to deny that the claims of lower-income and upper-middle-income students are now approaching a point of direct competition.

The recent Middle-Income Student Assistance Act is illustrative of the developing clash of interests. The Basic Grant program has been the most rapidly growing federal aid program since its enactment in 1972. Its basic concept is simple and workable—that aid should tend to equalize the financial resources available to families for education. The Carnegie Council has repeatedly urged that the program should have the

highest priority, and that it be made a better program by allowing awards to be calculated on the basis of the full amount of a
student's noninstructional costs without the present limitation
on awards to one half of costs.

But in the confusion created by the variety of ill-defined
and overlapping aid programs, it was not the desirability of
more adequate cost allowances for lower-income students that
attracted administrative and Congressional attention but rather
the ease with which the mechanisms of the program could be
adapted to provide grants to students from upper-middle-
income families whose parents were pressing for tax reduction.
As a result, program costs are to be increased dramatically without achieving any increase in the inadequate allowed costs of
attendance for lower-income students.

Certainly, the trend toward including students from higher
and higher income families among aid eligibles should now stop.
In 1979-80, typical students from families with $25,000 in in-
come will be eligible for Basic Grants. In the CSS/ACT system
the income level at which parental contributions are deemed to
cover expenses at a public four-year college has risen from
$15,750 in 1972-73 to $27,250 in 1978-79 (Figure 9, Section
4). We have reached a point where only families with $30,000
or more in income are generally expected to pay the full expenses of a child attending even a modestly expensive private
college. Even beyond this level of income, grants are sometimes
available and the family contribution can take the form of a
highly subsidized GSL loan. Adding tuition tax credits or flat
grants would be unnecessary, regressive, and strongly at odds
with the equal opportunity priorities of higher education and
the national society.

The priorities of a need-based system should not be further
relief of middle-income families as such but rather a set of
changes that would tend to equalize opportunity:

• More adequate recognition of the noninstructional costs of
attendance that all students face and that absorb a large part
of the expected family contributions of lower- and lower-
middle-income families. The Basic Grant program currently

recognizes noninstructional costs of only $1,500 (including room and board) for nonresidential students. College Entrance Examination Board survey data suggests that $2,400 would be a more realistic standard allowance, and this is incorporated in the Council Recommendation 5.

• Repeal of the limitation of a Basic Grant to one half of total costs of attendance. The limitation in practice restricts the grants only of lower-income students attending low-cost colleges. In its place there should be a standard earnings expectation applicable to students of all income levels and attending all types of institutions (Council Recommendations 1, 2, 3 and 6).

• Much higher appropriations for the State Student Incentive Grant program (Council Recommendation 11) in order to provide states with inadequate state scholarship programs—many of them poor states—an incentive for expanding them. States fully implementing an eligible program under the Council proposals would usually bring down the net costs for a lower-income student attending a residential state institution to roughly the same level as for attending a local community college. A lower-income student attending a private college would have available a state grant equal to more than half of the tuition charged by an average-cost private institution, greatly enhancing his or her range of choice.

Adequate funding for these improvements could be achieved by redistributing current funds that do not serve equal opportunity objectives at all well. Within the program structure of the U.S. Office of Education, changes in the student loans programs would release the most important amounts of funding. The kind of National Student Loan Bank proposed in Council Recommendation 13 would:

• Eliminate the need for interest subsidies. These subsidies are now awarded without regard to any means test in the GSL program.
• Make unnecessary the capital contributions that are now made to the National Direct Student Loan program.

• Reduce default costs drastically.

Federal funds now devoted to social security benefits and food stamps for college students would also be better spent in strengthening the need-based character of the student aid system. Recommendations 2 and 4 through 9, as well as 17 and 18, propose such reallocations.

There will be further opportunities for reallocation as the student aid system is adapted to demographic developments now beginning to affect the colleges. The overall decline in the numbers of young people of traditional college-going age—18 to 22—will not be accompanied by as much of a decrease in young people from lower-income families. Young people from poverty-level families will eventually comprise about 17 percent of all persons in the 18 to 22 age group. A reallocation of aid resources from the declining number of upper- and middle-income students to students from poor families can take place without any reduction in aid per student to the former group.

We are aware that reallocation of funds within the federal budget and from agency to agency is a painful and uncertain affair. Jurisdictional rivalries are not easily overcome. It is nonetheless worth pointing out that an aid system that would serve equal opportunity objectives better need not cost the taxpayer more. Table 1 (Section 1) provides an overall comparison of estimated federal expenditures under existing programs and Council recommendations.

12

Expanding
Student Choice

For a decade, much of the public policy debate concerning student aid has contrasted the objectives of "equal access" and "choice." More often than not the objective of access has been understood to be the goal of assuring a place in a low-cost college for every student seeking to enroll and enough money to meet the minimum expenses of attending such an institution.

"Choice," on the other hand, has tended to mean the lowering of financial obstacles to choosing a residential or high-tuition institution, usually a private institution, but often also an out-of-state public institution charging high tuition and fees to nonresidents.

Equal access and choice have often been discussed as though they were absolute standards against which the student aid system should be measured. If so, they are clearly conflicting standards. For no student aid system can make its maximum contribution to equal access unless all its resources are devoted to equalizing family financial resources for education, leaving nothing left over to reduce the financial obstacles to choice. In a system of higher education characterized by large differences in tuition and fee expenses at different institutions, achieving both perfect equality of access and perfect equality of choice must be illusory. It is far more useful to think of access and choice not as preemptive values but as goals which must be brought into balance.

Choice, in these terms, is of concern to public policy because the higher education system as a whole can be most effective only if there are mechanisms for matching students of differing educational needs and institutions with differing programs. If unequal costs of attendance impede this matching, student aid can play a role in making the educational system work better even as it extends the opportunities available to individual students.

The Terms of Choice

The amount of choice that exists is necessarily hard to measure empirically, since it is not so much a matter of what people decide to do but how constrained their decisions seem to them to be. We cannot even say much about how the factors in a decision to attend an expensive or inexpensive institution are weighed. The value of the education a student is expected to receive at an institution may be variously weighed against:

1. The gross charges of the institution
2. The charges net of financial aid
3. The out-of-pocket cost net of loans which must be repaid later
4. The difference in cost between an expensive institution and the least expensive alternative acceptable institution
5. The fraction of family income (or assets or acceptable indebtedness) represented by the cost difference between institutions

Some families probably make their decisions in each of these ways. Although some may appear generally better than others, there are arguments for each one of them being the best way in at least some cases.

We can say a little more—although with a considerable admixture of conjecture—about the aggregate result of the decisions families appear to be making currently:

• Private college enrollments in total have not recently dropped significantly, although private institutions in some categories, most clearly small Catholic institutions, have suffered badly.

- Private colleges have done a great deal to make themselves more attractive and better known, and have thereby sought to give more weight to what they have to offer in exchange for high tuition.
- Public institutions have, however, come to see themselves as also needing to compete for students, often adopting programs similar to those that make private colleges attractive or inaugurating their own improvements.
- The most selective institutions remain in great demand, despite what are usually the highest tuition levels (before deducting student aid). There is suggestive evidence that selectivity outweighs cost considerations for the brightest students, and that this effect is pronounced at all levels of income (Spies, 1978).
- Some lowering of admissions standards is occurring among many less prestigious selective institutions, opening up alternatives hitherto unavailable to families that can manage the financing.
- There is evidence that a central core of strong attachment to private institution alternatives accounts for substantial private college enrollments in states with traditionally large public sectors; but that private sectors are likely to experience declining enrollment in states with traditionally large private sectors, probably chiefly from segments of their populations whose preference for private higher education is not strong (Carnegie Council on Policy Studies in Higher Education, 1977).
- Students choosing private institutions appear more often to have made a firm prior decision not to enter the labor market immediately after high school, with the result that private institution enrollments seem to be less vulnerable to short-term changes in labor market conditions.
- Private colleges may, however, be relatively less attractive as families weigh costs of attendance against a perceived long-term decline in the economic value of education in general.
- The very high admissions standards of many graduate professional schools may be helping those private colleges that are perceived as increasing the chances of their graduates being admitted to such schools.

- A probable increase in reliance on students' own earnings in financing higher education may be to the disadvantage of many private colleges. Even if they are located in favorable labor markets, the fraction of total expenses a student can expect to earn will be less at these institutions.

These are some of the many cross-currents affecting choice of college.

Student Aid for Choice

Recent developments have affected the amount of student aid funds available to meet high tuition levels both positively and negatively. On the positive side, there has occurred rapid growth in state grant funds, often with the avowed intention of helping to close the "tuition gap." State aid, however, is still very unevenly distributed; five states still account for over 65 percent of all state funds. Moreover, state aid is seldom "portable" to an out-of-state institution. Lack of portability is in obvious conflict with the public policy rationale favoring choice.

Another positive factor is the rapid growth of institutional aid funds set aside from unrestricted revenues (including tuition revenues). And Basic Grants, although regarded as an "access" program, have provided a floor of support that has made it considerably easier for at least the less selective private colleges to build aid packages and to extend recruitment efforts among low-income and minority students.

On the negative side, student aid officers at public institutions have increased competition for federal "campus-based" student aid. This competition, together with inflation, has meant that many private colleges have less aid to award from these sources in constant dollars than they had in the early 1970s, despite rising federal appropriations.

The Relative Specificity of Aid

Another development may be of roughly equal importance to these changes in the sources and amounts of aid supporting choice. In the early 1970s, most aid was distributed through the student aid officer's packaging process. Aid funds were unevenly matched with aggregate need from institution to institution, but the packaging process uniformly had the effect of treating one dollar of student need as having an equal *prima facie* claim to aid as any other, whether subsistence costs or tuition costs represented the greater part of a student's budget. There was no bias in the packaging approach against obtaining aid to meet high tuition costs, and no greater convenience or reliability to obtaining aid to meet subsistence costs.

This situation has changed markedly. The rapid growth of the Basic Grant program has meant that aid toward meeting half of allowed costs of attendance up to $3,600 (twice the maximum Basic Grant of $1,800) is relatively much easier to get and relatively assured. These very desirable features of the Basic Grant program have, for lack of equivalent features in most aid programs helping students pay higher levels of expense, inadvertently biased the distribution process (as distinct from any bias in the allocation of funds) in favor of public institutions. This effect results from the fact that a Basic Grant award covers a larger fraction of total expenses at institutions whose total costs of attendance are in the range typical for public institutions than in the range typical for private institutions. Since a larger proportion of total costs at most public institutions represents subsistence than at private institutions, the advent of the Basic Grant program also can be seen as making aid to attend a public institution or to meet subsistence costs relatively more predictable, reliable, and simple to obtain than aid to meet tuition costs—at least those of most private institutions. This situation constricts choice even though the Basic Grant program has helped private institutions stretch their discretionary aid resources and appears to have helped recruitment at the less selective private institutions.

Council Recommendations 11 through 13 would increase student aid resources for choice and also the predictability of aid for choice. They propose:

- Expansion of need-based state grant programs, operating on the entitlement principle
- An additional matching incentive to encourage interstate portability of state grants

• Establishment of a National Student Loan Bank to assure students a reliable source of borrowing to meet tuition costs
• Continuation of the SEOG program

A reasonable degree of choice would thus be assured independently of the availability of discretionary institutional funds through the student aid officer of a particular institution, although such resources would continue to play a role.

Under these proposals, however, there would not be an attempt to make the choice between a low- and a high-tuition institution neutral in determining financial obligations. Parents would be expected to pay more toward an expensive education if they could. Students would be expected to increase their self-help contribution, through additional earnings or loan obligations or both. The proportions of total costs of attendance met by public resources, on the one hand, and by parental contributions, student earnings, and loans, on the other, would vary with out of pocket costs as illustrated in Figure 24.

The additional burdens of attending a high tuition institution would, however, be certain and manageable in size and form. We believe that, in the conditions created by implementation of our proposals, families could fairly weigh educational alternatives without excluding high-tuition colleges on the basis of cost alone, and institutions could engage in fair and productive educational competition.

This new degree of support for choice could be provided without major increases in federal or state funds. This results from use of assured private borrowing from an efficient National Student Loan Bank to cover important amounts of tuition expenses at private institutions, as well as from discontinuation of Social Security benefits and food stamps for college students.

Figure 24. Typical public and private shares of cost of attendance
under proposals

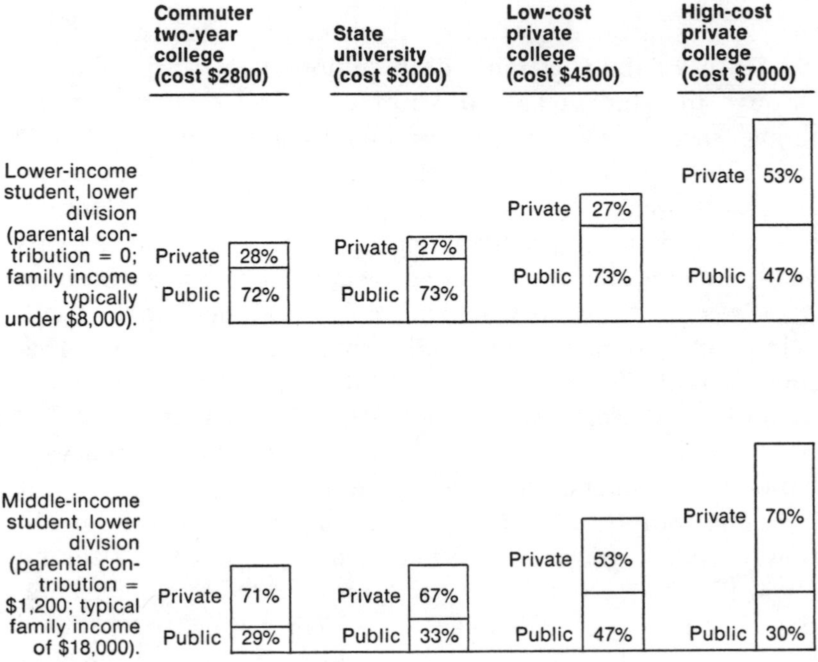

Source: Carnegie Council staff estimates.

13

Improving the Student Loan System

No student aid program has been the subject of more adverse comment than the federal Guaranteed Student Loan (GSL) program. The leading cause of criticism is, of course, its very high default rates. A second frequent cause of criticism has been use of the program by some proprietary schools to finance students whose tuition payments they were glad to have but whom they were ill-prepared to teach. Beginning in 1975 and 1976 steps were taken to exclude less reputable proprietary schools from the program, and the result has been a gratifying fall in default rates. The students whose loans are now coming due for repayment are much less likely to have been students who enrolled in questionable schools, and, it appears, are more often willing to repay their loans. The U.S. Office of Education has also required lenders to adopt more energetic collection practices, under pain of loss of the federal loan guarantee. Borrowers whose loans have passed into federal hands after default has occurred are being pressed aggressively to begin payments. Receipts from such defaulting borrowers have climbed rapidly.

However, the default problem has not by any means gone away. The historical rate of defaults—over the life of the program—is perhaps 13.5 percent. The default rate on loans currently coming due for repayment is lower—perhaps as low as 10 percent. But some factors contributing to defaults are likely to be less tractable than was the excessive use of the program by proprietary schools. If default rates on the order of 10 percent are unacceptable, new approaches to the problem should be considered. The relatively much lower delinquency rates on other types of loans make it clear that the problems underlying collection of student loans must be especially severe (Table 24):

Table 24. Delinquency rates by type of credit, July 1978

	Percentage of loans
FHA home improvement and mobile home loan	4.0
Automobile loans	1.7
Personal loans	3.2
Credit cards	2.2

Source: American Bankers Association, 1978.

Problems of Students, Lenders, and Aid Officers

The default problem has been of so much concern that it has at times diverted attention from other problems of the loan programs. Students have often been unable to find willing lenders. Lenders have often been unable to keep track of loans and borrowers, and often have been discouraged about participation in the programs by both the inherent difficulties of managing a portfolio of student loans and by changing regulations. Student aid officers have been unsure whether student loans could be counted on as part of individual aid packages. Tax payers may begin to notice, more than in the past, rapid increases in the interest subsidy costs of the GSL appearing in the federal budget.

None of these problems is unrelated to each of the others because the present program reflects questionable choices about how to make credit available to students in a form they can use to finance college expenses. These choices have dictated the mechanisms that have proved troublesome.

Reliance on Commercial Lenders

The first such choice was that private commercial lenders ordinarily should provide the capital to lend to students, should review individual loan applications, and should collect the loans they had made. Their role was, then, conceived to be similar to the one they assume in other lending activities. But, from the first, it was seen that the incentives operating on lenders in their usual role could be at odds with some of the objectives of public policy for student loans. Good lending practice would dictate that loans be limited to students who could provide security in the form of pledged assets or, in the alternative, could be certified as good credit risks. But many low-income students would be unable to meet either requirement. Without special intervention, a commercial student loan program would be likely to make credit available to those who needed it relatively least.

The Federal Guarantee

The purpose of the federal guarantee of student loans (or federal reinsurance in the case of student loans guaranteed by state agencies) was to overcome this problem. Lenders would not be forced to discriminate against low-income students because a federal guarantee would guard them against risk of default as well as a pledge.

However, a federal guarantee is too good a substitute for security in one respect. It invites lenders to rely entirely on the government's promise to cover losses. By eliminating the risks of default, it deprives the lender of any incentive to try to make the borrower repay. Lax collection efforts can result. In the last few years this problem has been resolved by requiring lenders to engage in specific collection activities and by refusing to honor guarantees where there has been a lack of "due diligence" in collections. But performing the required collection activities has increased the lenders' costs of servicing loans. Lenders have been compensated for these costs by increases in a "Special Allowance" subsidy on outstanding credit, but this allowance has also had to compensate them for the higher costs of money induced by inflation. Subsidy increases have tended to lag behind increases in the regulatory burden (*Report to the Congress . . .* , 1977).

Lenders have been discouraged by both declining net yield and impairment of the federal guarantee. In other words, efforts to overcome the problem created by the guarantee being too good a substitute for ordinary collateral have made it not quite good enough for some lenders. As a result, there may now be an increasing tendency for lenders to act more on their normal inclination to favor borrowers with good credit ratings—which the federal guarantee was to repress. If that is so, improvements in the default rate could result, but at the cost of reduced access to loans for lower-income borrowers.

The Problem of Tracing Borrowers

There is one respect in which the government's guarantee is no substitute for conventional collateral. An important fact about the kinds of assets ordinarily accepted as collateral is that lenders know where they are. The lender knows where the mortgaged house is located and will continue to be located. He knows also where pledged securities and property titles are located—somewhere under his own lock and key. The borrower also has an interest in the collateral pledged and the convergence of the creditor's and debtor's interests means that the one can usually find the other. Not so with GSL loans. The official certification of the federal guarantee gives no clue about where the borrower can be found. Tracing borrowers can be a major problem for lenders who are trying to collect. The federal government has its own system for tracing people, namely social security and withholding tax files, but this system is not available to commercial lenders until a default has already occurred and has been made good by the federal government. At that point, the U.S. Office of Education can use federal tracing resources to try to find the borrower.

The Scarcity of Loan Funds

Another potential problem arising from the decision to rely on private lenders to make student loans is that they simply may not have funds they want to lend to students, or not enough to meet recognized student need. Banks must consider how much it would cost them to increase their aggregate lendable funds and what the comparative risk and yield of lending to students rather than to other kinds of borrowers might be. Most banks have regarded student loans as most similar to consumer installment loans and seem to have had this analogy in mind in deciding on the proportion of their lending that should be channeled into student loans and in deciding whether they are a relatively worthwhile type of business. Their decisions on these points have often meant that less funds were available than students sought.

One attempt to deal with these problems occurred in 1972 when the Congress chartered the Student Loan Marketing Association (Sallie Mae) to raise capital for student loans either directly from private sources or *via* the Federal Financing Bank (which has become the standard practice). Sallie Mae has the potential, only now being realized operationally, of offering lenders capital at relatively low cost through mechanisms that largely eliminate competition for lendable funds between student loans and other borrowing. Banks have, however, been slow to take advantage of Sallie Mae programs, and this suggests that there must be doubts whether Sallie Mae operations will in fact provide assured access to loans on a routine basis and throughout the country at any time in the next few years, although Sallie Mae operations could, in principle, assure a flow of loan funds adequate to student needs.

There have also been unsanctioned mechanisms to induce additional lending. If the ultimate provider of loan capital is relieved of the obligation of servicing the loans made with its funds, its net yield can be almost as high as its gross yield from subsidies and student interest payments. Schools have sometimes been willing to absorb servicing costs in order to provide an incentive of higher yield to induce banks or others to provide loan capital. A variety of mechanisms can be used to achieve the desired result. But they can weaken a weak school financially and can result in lax or incompetent collection efforts. There have been instances of fraud against students associated with such schemes and the Office of Education has forbidden or greatly restricted most of the available mechanisms of this sort.

The Problem of Repayment

A second basic decision that has caused problems for the GSL program was to prescribe a short repayment period of ten years and to provide that repayment normally be in equal installments. This decision means that borrowers are expected to amortize the educational investments of a lifetime over the same period they might need to finance two or three successive automobiles. Students' ability to manage debt service is greatly constrained, especially since in the years immediately after leaving college graduates are likely to earn lower incomes than graduates later in life. Limiting in this way the amount of debt student borrowers will be able to repay both restricts the role that self-help can play in financing education and makes it more likely that students will default on loans.

Interest Subsidies

The difficulty students would have in paying off educational loans in ten years would be considerably greater if interest charges while students are still in college were added to the principal amount owed and became the basis for additional interest charges. One of the reasons the Congress enacted a system of interest subsidies for the program was to keep periodic repayment burdens within bounds, despite the ten-year repayment period. Interest charges are payed currently and by the federal government while the student borrower remains in school, avoiding the need to compound interest.

Interest subsidies have certainly achieved this intended purpose, but they have become an additional source of problems. The cost to taxpayers has been high and, with the recent elimination of all income tests for eligibility for the subsidies, may mount rapidly higher. The actual value of the subsidy to students increases with the amount they borrow and the length of time they take to repay, not with the amount of the student's need. It has therefore become obvious to some students and parents that a benefit is to be reaped from borrowing even if family resources are ample, just for the sake of the subsidy. A student who borrows the maximum allowed amount as an undergraduate, and who has no need for the funds, could invest them in 9 percent certificates of deposit and legally gain $2,200 in interest. If he or she went on to a three-year graduate program, the gain could be $7,525. If lendable funds are in short supply, as they have tended to be, and if the lender preference for credit-worthy borrowers is not completely repressed by the federal guarantee, then the availability of the interest subsidy has almost certainly diverted some student loan funds away from meeting student need.

Finally, the terms of the interest subsidy have made adequate record keeping almost impossible and, because of inadequate records, have increased defaults. This is because a lender trying to keep track of a loan must not only keep track of where the student is (which we have seen is difficult enough) but also of the stages of his or her career. It is graduating or dropping out of school that ordinarily triggers the ending—nine months later—of eligibility for continuing interest subsidies and the beginning of the obligation to make repayments. If the lender does not know when such events occur—and it is against the interest of the borrower to inform the lender—then a loan can slip into delinquency and default without the lender even knowing it. By the time the lender finds out, the borrower may be far away or may have got in the habit of thinking that loan repayments can be avoided.

The Pattern of Proliferating Complexity

The foregoing is a very incomplete account of the actions taken to solve the problems of the GSL program without departing from the initial decisions to rely on commercial lenders and to require repayment over a short period. Regulations on student, lender, and aid officer conduct are extraordinarily detailed. A series of very complicated and expensive centralized and decentralized record-keeping systems have been built, only to fail in providing critical information when it will do the most good. Special regulations and policies apply to purchases and sales of loans, to collaboration between lenders and colleges, to colleges acting as lenders, and to excessive dependence of schools on financing tuition through loans. These regulations have been thought necessary to forestall the proliferation of abuse.

Perhaps, however, enough has been said to indicate that further tinkering with the program is unlikely to solve the problems encountered. The solutions adopted have generally led to further problems and also to increased costs—borne, in the main, by federal taxpayers.

The National Direct Student Loan Program

The smaller National Direct Student Loan (NDSL) program operates on a different set of assumptions than the GSL program. A college, not a bank, typically makes the loan. Ninety percent of lendable funds are provided by federal appropriations. As a result, lenders are eager to make loans, and do not need federal guarantees or subsidies to encourage them to do so. In the NDSL program it is solely the student (rather than the lender and the student, as in GSL) who is subsidized. The student's subsidy is not paid annually by a special federal payment but is implicit in the very low interest charged—none while enrolled or in certain kinds of service and 3 percent thereafter. It is a real subsidy nonetheless. From the taxpayers' point of view, it can be calculated as the difference, on 90 percent of each loan, between the programs' average interest rate of less than 3 percent and the Federal Treasury's borrowing rate. The college also subsidizes the student to the extent of absorbing most costs of originating and servicing loans, and also by the difference, on 10 percent of the loan, between the low NDSL interest rates and the yield the college could get from an alternative investment.

These subsidies are undesirable. They do not complicate the task of keeping track of the student as much as those of the GSL program do, because the lender, which is the college, knows when the student graduates or withdraws. But they are obviously unfair to students who do not receive them, and who must make use of GSL loans instead, with their much lower rate of subsidy. The NDSL subsidies do not generally operate to increase unnecessary borrowing for the sake of the subsidy, since student aid officers ordinarily ration scarce NDSL funds quite restrictively. But once a student has received an NDSL loan, he or she is likely to take as long as possible to repay. For most of the past decade, the rate of inflation (and also savings account interest rates) have far exceeded the 3 percent NDSL rate. Thus, it pays for the student to delay repayment. This has tended to be easy since student aid officers have authority under the legislation to postpone or stretch out the student's repayment period, and have often been glad to do so, either out of generous feelings toward student borrowers or to avoid the embarrassment of having to count loans as in default.

The overall picture on collections of NDSL loans is not clear, but it is obviously not good. Delinquency and default rates used to be calculated in a way that made these rates seem less than those for the GSL program. On a comparable basis the historical default rate—over the life of the NDSL program—is perhaps 19 percent. This is somewhat worse than the GSL rate. It might have been slightly better if the U.S. Office of Education had moved all along—as it now intends—to exclude colleges with very bad rates. Some 200 institutions have historical default rates of more than 50 perent, whereas the better institutions—1,100 of them—have rates of under 10 percent. Colleges, can, and often do, use commercial collection agencies to service their NDSL portfolios, so the lack of professionalism of colleges in collection procedures can be remedied.

Fundamental Problems of Both Programs

In the end, the fundamental problems of assuring repayment are the same for both the NDSL and GSL programs and this suggests that the lowest feasible default rates will still be high for both. Both borrower populations include highly mobile individuals, often from poor families, who do not always see the importance of maintaining good credit ratings. In neither case do borrowers risk their own collateral. The advantages of using government collection resources rather than private ones are therefore the same for both populations. Table 25 shows historical percentages of GSL defaults by family income and by type of control of college. The higher default rates of lower-income students and of institutions with greater proportions of lower-income students suggests how difficult it is bound to be to have low default rates in a loan program serving lower-income students without strengthened collection mechanisms.

Table 25. Percentage of defaults compared with percentage of loans under the federal Guaranteed Student Loan program and guarantee agency programs, by family income of student and by type and control of institution attended, fiscal years 1966-1974

Family income and type and control of institution	Guaranteed Student Loan program			Guarantee agency programs[b]		
	Percentage of defaults (1)	Percentage of loans (2)	Ratio of (1) to (2)	Percentage of defaults (1)	Percentage of loans (2)	Ratio of (1) to (2)
Adjusted family income[a]						
$0 to $3,000	47.6%	29.3%	1.6	27.3%	15.4%	1.8
$3,000 to 6,000	21.5	23.0	0.9	25.3	20.7	1.2
$6,000 to 9,000	10.5	17.1	0.6	19.6	23.3	0.8
$9,000 to 12,000	4.8	10.2	0.5	12.7	19.2	0.7
$12,000 to 15,000	1.8	5.1	0.4	6.4	2.7	2.4
More than $15,000	0.8	1.9	0.4	1.2	2.7	0.4
Income not available	13.1	13.4	1.0	7.4	6.6	1.1
Type of college						
Colleges and universities	28.2	48.3	0.6	67.0	81.3	0.8
Junior colleges and institutes	10.4	7.2	1.4	16.3	10.5	1.6
Specialized vocational	59.7	37.2	1.6	15.0	6.0	2.5
Not classified	1.8	7.3	0.2	1.6	2.2	0.7
Control of college						
Public	31.7	47.5	0.7	47.4	54.1	0.9
Private	8.6	14.6	0.6	37.6	38.9	1.0
Proprietary	59.2	36.2	1.6	14.7	5.9	2.5
Not classified	0.5	1.7	0.3	0.2	1.1	0.2

[a]Adjusted family income (used in determining eligibility for the interest subsidy) represents 90 percent of family income less federal income tax exemptions.

[b]Chiefly state agencies with loans reinsured by the federal government.

Source: Hauptman (1977, pp. 141-142).

Tinkering Versus Thorough Reform

The recommendations we make for establishing a National Student Loan Bank assume a different set of fundamental decisions about providing credit to finance college attendance. We believe that the following principles are fundamental:

1. Access to loans must be assured.
2. It must be possible to coordinate eligibility for loans with other aid.
3. Borrowers must be put in a position such that they can and will repay their loans.

These principles do not necessarily require that commercial lenders have no role in making student loans, nor do they require that new sources of loan capital be tapped. But the first principle does mean that commercial lenders should not be put in the position of having to ration loan funds. The amount of the loan a student receives should be determined by student aid officers according to the ground rules for coordination of aid from all sources. This means that government credit, whether in the form of Treasury borrowing or guarantees of Sallie Mae borrowing, would almost certainly have to play a larger role than at present, and incentives to involve the regular capital sources of commercial lenders a lesser role. It also means that an adequate system for assuring repayment, as required by the third principle, should not rest, if it ever could, on ordinary collection efforts by originating commercial lenders.

Some features of a National Student Loan Bank could be grafted on to the present system. But if this is done, the complexity of present inadequate solutions to the problems of the program should not be allowed to stand in the way of achieving fundamental reforms. We think the arguments are strong for starting afresh with an entirely new program. Even if this is not done, changes should not be undertaken in a spirit of further tinkering. Solutions that have been tried and have not worked very well should be replaced and not merely elaborated further.

A National Student Loan Bank

Accordingly, Council Recommendation 13 proposes that the federal government charter a new National Student Loan Bank, a nonprofit private corporation to be financed by the sale of governmentally guaranteed securities. This is how Sallie Mae has obtained capital and it would be possible to convert Sallie Mae into a loan bank. It would be necessary however:

1. To buy out owners of Sallie Mae shares
2. To authorize Sallie Mae to originate student loans and build up an organization to do so
3. To change the mode of Sallie Mae operations from one of negotiated purchases and warehousing facilities to one of general and direct student access

If our recommendations concerning the Basic Grant program, federal/state tuition grants, and Work-Study were fully implemented, the need to borrow from a National Student Loan Bank would be limited to those students who attended high tuition institutions or who were unable to find jobs consistent with their academic obligations or whose parents could, but do not for one reason or another, meet the specified contribution rates. Operating in a context of adequate and coordinated grant programs and in the absence of interest subsidies tending to induce unnecessary borrowing, the total volume of loan demand could be much less than under present ground rules.

From the point of view of the borrower seeking a loan, a National Student Loan Bank would mainly have the effect of making it clear where the student could turn to be assured of getting funds. The now frequent situation of having to shop from bank to bank with no assurance of success would no longer occur.

The nature of the student's repayment obligation and its implications would, however, change more drastically. The student could no longer expect to enjoy heavily subsidized interest rates. Interest at rates slightly higher than Federal Treasury long-term borrowing costs (to cover the bank's cost of money) would be compounded until the student's studies and any period of military or volunteer service were completed. The student, therefore, would not be tempted to borrow more than necessary for the sake of interest subsidy benefits. But, at the same time, the borrower would be put in the position of knowing that repayment of necessary debt would be manageable, since repayment could be over a much longer period—on average, 20 years—and annual installments would be geared to current income. At the same time, there would be no prospect of evading the stipulated obligations once undertaken.

The Internal Revenue Service (IRS) has traditionally opposed use of its tax collection mechanisms to recover other debts to the federal government or to administer social programs in the way proposed for the National Student Loan Bank. The line drawn by the IRS has, however, clearly been breached in the case of the low-income tax credit, which is a form of income maintenance. The arguments for a further exception in the case of student loans are strong. Student loans are unique, or nearly so, in requiring a commitment of federal credit without collateral other than the incomes student borrowers will eventually earn and the IRS will monitor. The only alternative to IRS collection of student loans that comes even close to equivalent effectiveness would be for a National Student Loan Bank to have routine access to the tracing facilities of the IRS whenever initial efforts of the bank to pursue borrowers fail. This approach would mean a common borrower information system although collection agencies would be separate.

Fundamental Choices

A National Student Loan Bank would represent a clear alternative to the present Guaranteed Loan Program. The bank's sources of capital would be very like those of Sallie Mae. But gone would be reliance on a federal guarantee of each student loan in order to induce lending to low-income borrowers. Gone would be the apparatus of regulations, penalties, and subsidies to induce lenders to engage in aggressive loan servicing practices. Gone would be interest subsidies to students to reduce the burden of amortizing loans over a short period. Gone would be the temptation to unnecessary borrowing created by interest subsidies. Gone would be the major obstacles to collection efforts.

A National Student Loan Bank would provide alternative solutions to the basic problems of loan availability and repayment. It would make unnecessary the complications that have flowed from the additional problems created by the old solutions. Now that efforts to eliminate the scandals that have plagued the program are proving successful, it is a good time to reassess the basic choices that have governed the structure of the program. Quite aside from abuse and scandal, the mechanisms of the program have simply not been very appropriate. The alternative of a National Student Loan Bank should be seriously debated.

14

Aiding Adult, Part-Time, and Independent Students

A growing proportion of total enrollments consists of adults, part-time students, and independent students whose parents are determined to have no obligation to provide them with financial support. The kinds of programs in which these various students participate are highly varied, ranging from remedial education through work toward a regular first degree to postprofessional and avocational programs of "lifelong learning." The participation of such individuals in the student aid system should be along lines that assure fairness, consistency with the treatment of traditional students, and avoidance of bias that would arbitrarily favor one form of educational participation over another.

Figure 25 provides a taxonomy of the cases with which public policy must be prepared to deal. The figure does, however, conceal an important premise that should be made explicit. There are no cells in the figure designated according to the age of the student. This reflects the premise that differences in the ages of students do not, by themselves, indicate the appropriateness of differences of treatment in the student aid system. Rather, the age of students has a bearing on the likelihood that they will choose one pattern of enrollment rather than another, that they will have been self-supporting for some

Figure 25. Traditional and "nontraditional" students

	Dependent Students		Independent Students	
	Single	Having family responsibilities	Single	Having family responsibilities
Full-time students	("Traditional" students)			
Part-time students				

time, that their earning capacities will be different, and that they will have family responsibilities of their own.

The Varied Situations of Part-Time Students

The rapid growth of part-time enrollments in recent years has raised questions about the treatment of part-time students in aid programs. Much of the growth has resulted from two factors working together: rising educational aspirations among adults and the greater accessibility of institutions near where adults live and work. Another factor has been the return of veterans from the Vietnam war who are entitled by law to substantial G.I. Bill benefits. There have also been new patterns of college attendance among students of traditional college-going age, 18 to 22, who have chosen to spend a greater part of these years in jobs and other pursuits and relatively less in the classroom.

Financial considerations of one kind or another are an important motive for many decisions in favor of part-time enrollment. Such a decision can represent an individual solution to the basic problem student aid programs address—how to find

enough money to live and attend college—since part-time enrollment permits commitment of more time to employment and
higher earnings than full-time students can usually achieve. In
other cases a full-time job coupled with part-time enrollment
makes possible a higher standard of living for the student than
he or she could otherwise enjoy. In still other cases, it is the
need to provide support to others—to parents, siblings, spouse,
or children—that enjoins the choice of part-time enrollment.

Because part-time students include so many individuals
who are making serious efforts to solve their own financial
problems or who are taking their family responsibilities seriously, the student aid system should take them seriously also.
But this does not mean that part-time students should necessarily receive a share of student aid funds equal to their share of
all enrollments or even of full-time equivalent enrollments.
There is no practical alternative to assessing the financial need
of part-time students on a case-by-case basis. If the financial
need of a part-time student is less because he or she devotes
more time to paid employment, then that fact should be taken
as given by the student aid system, even if the student's earnings
have the effect of reducing his or her student aid awards. To
attempt to do otherwise would involve the student aid system
in trying to extricate all the motives for choosing part-time
enrollment and to say how much of the student's earnings
should be attributed to each of them.

However, there is a need here—and in dealing with independent students also, who may or may not be enrolled part-
time—for discretionary student aid funds to deal with special
circumstances. Part-time study does not always have the financial advantage of permitting higher earnings. Handicapped students may enroll part-time because their problems of daily living barely permit such enrollment, let alone time to spare for
employment. Mothers may find that part-time enrollment does
not enable them to resolve problems of childcare without paying for additional services. Some students choose part-time
enrollment who need more time to prepare for each course because of inadequate academic background. Simple and general
programs of student aid cannot take into account all the com-

plexities and nuances of such situations. Discretionary aid, such as we have proposed be available through the SEOG program and through special funding equal to 10 percent of regular Basic Grant funds, should be available to deal with these cases.

General Rules for Part-Time Students

The simplest set of situations for which general rules need to be developed are those of single, part-time, dependent students. Their tuition costs are generally less than those of full-time students, although not always proportional to their reduced course loads. Their subsistence costs are indistinguishable from those of full-time students. Their earning opportunities, however, are generally greater, because more of their time is available for employment—which, indeed, can often be in full-time jobs. Putting these characteristics together suggests that an appropriate general rule would be to expect a larger earnings contribution from such students. For example, as a standard minimum, this additional earnings expectation for half-time students might be set at half the cost of standard noninstructional costs ($1,200). Their regular self-help contribution toward such costs should, however, be reduced *pro rata*—from $600 or $1,000 to $300 or $500. Students enrolled more than half-time but less than full-time would be treated similarly but with different *pro rata* adjustments. Students whose enrollment is less than half-time would ordinarily not need a grant toward noninstructional costs, for these are students with sufficient time to commit to fully self-supporting employment. A student employed half-time at the current minimum wage would earn over $2,500 during an academic year of 40 weeks, thereby meeting the noninstructional costs the Basic Grant program should cover. Exceptional cases where a student cannot be expected to earn such an amount should be dealt with under discretionary programs, rather than in the regular Basic Grant program.

This approach would provide smaller Basic Grants to part-time students enrolled half-time or more than does the present calculation, which does not take account of additional earning opportunities to the same degree. For example, a student attending college half-time whose parents are expected to contribute $1,000 would now receive a grant of $400—half of the difference between $1,800 and the expected family contribution. Under the proposed rules the same student would receive no grant, because the sum of parental contribution ($1,000), half the regular self-help contribution ($300 or $500), and additional self-help ($1,200) would exceed $2,400.

Independent Students

It is far more difficult to devise general rules for independent students, whether full- or part-time. Becoming independent of one's parents is part of assuming the position of an adult in American society. The process of becoming thus independent is a topic of serious study for the social sciences. In the student aid system, however, the independence of a student has a different and narrower operational significance. A determination that a particular student is independent establishes that his or her case is to be treated as an exception to the general rule that parents are expected to provide whatever financial support they can.

This operational significance of independence is worth emphasizing because other and quite different concepts of independence—as a status, as an attitude, as a way of living, or as a mode of social participation—tend to creep inappropriately into criteria of independence for student aid purposes. But these concepts confuse the issue. The issue of which students are independent is simply the issue of which parents should not be expected to contribute to meeting educational expenses.

Public policy toward students who are independent in this sense encounters different problems depending on whether students are single or whether they have families of their own. To put the point very crudely, the problem with single independent students is to determine who they are. Once this is done, it is relatively easy to decide how they should be treated by the student aid system. The situation with independent students who have assumed family responsibilities of their own is almost exactly the opposite. It is easy to determine who they are, but it is difficult to decide how the student aid system should deal with their situations.

It is probably desirable to regard having a spouse or child as conclusive evidence of independence, at least for older students. With the possibility that one or both partners will have substantial earnings, the extent of the financial responsibility of each partner's parents, if any, becomes hard for the parties themselves, let alone for the administrators of the student aid system, to fix. There would be at least three family budgets to take into account if such students were not regarded as independent. There might well be an exception, however, in the case of students of traditional college-going age (under 22). It may be desirable to assume that the partner of a younger student cannot make a net contribution to the student's educational expenses, and that man, woman, and any offspring must look to the parents of both partners for support if their own earnings are inadequate. That is, a younger student even with family responsibilities should be treated by the aid system just as though he or she were a single dependent student. This is perhaps the only way to make the treatment of young students a neutral factor in decisions to form families.

Older students who are determined to be independent because they have family responsibilities of their own may be wage earners, homemakers, or both. Their academic commitments may require relinquishing these roles altogether, somewhat, or not at all, with varying consequences for their ability to finance educational expenses. This is why it is so difficult to arrive at appropriate rules for their treatment, even though the determination of their independent status is relatively easy. Their costs of attendance other than tuition are hard to extricate from the costs of supporting their families. It is arguable that they have either greater or lesser claims on the total resources (including credit resources) of their families than do dependent children. The families of such students may be recipients of unearned transfer payments that complicate analysis of their situations.

In dealing with these complexities, two premises are helpful:

• First, it is not appropriate to increase the size of aid packages received by such students in order to help them meet the subsistence costs of their dependents or the higher costs associated with the typical standard of living of adults living as a family unit, as opposed to the lower one typical of single students. Such a development would move the focus of student aid programs away from a proper focus on educational opportunity in the direction of a much less specific concern with income maintenance as such, where other public programs should take the lead.[1]

Second, it is not appropriate for the student aid system to compensate for the opportunity costs of withdrawal from other activities that study entails, except to the extent that this withdrawal reduces the net cash contribution a student can make toward educational expenses from his or her own earnings.

The statement of the first of these two premises speaks for itself. The second requires some additional explanation. For most adults, the additional outlays entailed by enrollment in higher education are mostly for tuition charges representing a small fraction of family income. For them, the largest practical obstacle to obtaining additional education is not the problem of financing instructional costs, but rather the opportunity costs of doing without income that adult employment would otherwise continue to provide or the cost of purchasing homemaking services adults would otherwise provide to their families without cash payment. Traditional full-time modes of participation in higher education force extremely costly choices in these areas.

Younger students also incur opportunity costs in choosing higher education, but the sacrifices entailed are usually much smaller. As a result, a student aid system can be well adapted to the needs of younger students if it deals effectively with the problem of instructional and subsistence costs, even though it ignores opportunity costs. Such a system is perhaps even

[1]The argument here is that aid should not be awarded to cover subsistence costs of family members who are not themselves students. However, it would remain appropriate to exempt other income of the student and the student's partner from the means test assessment to allow for the subsistence costs of family members who are not students. Nonstudent family members have valid claim on these private resources.

strengthened by the fact that, for most younger students, their willingness to forego other opportunities for the sake of education provides an important assurance that they are serious about their educational objectives.

In the case of older students, however, opportunity costs are a major barrier. Yet public subsidies to compensate for them would be extremely expensive, difficult to reconcile with desirable employment incentives, difficult to design so that abuse could be prevented, and hard to square with the egalitarian premises of most contemporary social policy. And whereas an adequate system of aid to meet the costs of single dependent students becomes less expensive as society gets richer (because parents and students themselves can pay an increasing share of such costs), a program to compensate for opportunity costs becomes more expensive, since returns to alternative activities become greater.

For all of these reasons, the major contribution of public programs to resolving the opportunity costs problems posed by adult and continuing education may be to provide support for educational programs designed to minimize opportunity costs, rather than to compensate for them. Part-time and extension programs are the obvious vehicle for such efforts. Public support for their enrichment, greater educational effectiveness, and wider recognition may well be a more valid way of aiding recurrent education than subsidies to students.

If, then, public student aid programs should neither meet the subsistence needs of a student's dependents, nor compensate for all the opportunity costs of being a student, a reasonable rule for student aid benefits to independent students having family responsibilities can perhaps be specified. It would be to estimate first a family contribution equal to the parental contribution the family would be expected to make on behalf of a dependent student if family income were less by the amount of a standard student earnings contribution. This amount plus the earnings contribution could then be compared to cost of attendance to find need. Calculating the family and earnings contributions in this way would avoid assessing the earnings contribution twice—both in full and at the usual contribution rate.

However, a student aid officer should be able to make an extra grant to supplement aid calculated in this way in order to compensate for a projected loss of income because of academic obligations and for any projected increase in costs of home-maker services. These adjustments should not be allowed to yield a negative amount for the individual earnings contribution, because to do so would, in effect, provide support to the student's dependents. In the interests of keeping the rules of general federal and state entitlement programs relatively simple, these adjustments should only be made on a case-by-case basis by a student aid officer. Any increment in aid eligibility resulting from them should be met with discretionary funds—from SEOG funds, the proposed set-aside equal to 10 percent of Basic Grant entitlements, or institutional funds.

Under this approach three full-time students with standard noninstructional costs ($2,400) and tuition costs of $600, and identical family income situations before enrollment would be treated as shown in Table 26.

Table 26. Treatment of three hypothetical cases using one suggested approach for assisting independent students

	"Traditional" upper-division full-time student	*Previous full-time homemaker now needing to hire such services*	*Sole wage earner losing $2,000 in income because of reduced employment*
Family contribution	$ 200	$ 200	$ 0
Earnings	1,250	0	0
Basic Grant	1,200	1,200	1,400
Tuition grant	350	350	350
Discretionary grant	0	1,250	1,250
Total budget	$3,000	$3,000	$3,000

The needs of part-time independent students having family responsibilities would, of course, need to be considered through a combination of the approaches outlined here. Their part-time enrollment would, however, reduce their opportunity costs drastically, and they might often be capable of making the same contribution from earnings that a "traditional" dependent student would be expected to make.

Single Independent Students

An appropriate treatment for single independent students does not have to deal with similar complexities. If parental resources are, by definition, to be disregarded in assessing their ability to pay, then available parental resources are necessarily zero. Students who are independent in this sense should be treated just as dependent students whose parental resources available for education are assessed but are calculated to be zero. If they are part-time students, only the estimate of the contribution from their own earnings need be adjusted—just as it would be adjusted in the case of dependent part-time students.

This treatment is obviously valid, however, only for those students whose independence is not to some extent an artifact of student aid rules—namely, orphans. In other cases, if a disregard of parental resources increases the calculated deficit in funds available to the student to pay for education, it is because public policy chooses to say that children in these cases have no claim on their parents, although a calculation based on parental resources could be made.

There is no easy way to determine a consensus, if there is one, on which single students should be considered to have no such claim. However, student aid officers have thought about the problem more than anyone else, and most of them would probably be uncomfortable about criteria of independence that did not accord such status in at least clear cases where parental responsibility has already been "drawn down" in the past or has atrophied because the children have not needed to call on parental resources for some time, the children having been fully self-supporting. But even if we can assume such a consensus, translating it into administrative criteria is still difficult for several reasons:

1. Any set of criteria will seem unfair when applied to some

factual situations. There will be "borderline cases" and "hard cases."

2. It is desirable that the criteria chosen rely on the most relevant and conclusive information. But it is also desirable that verification be a fairly simple matter and that it not involve intrusive inquiries into the private affairs of parents and children. These considerations must conflict to some degree.

3. Although it is easy, as pointed out before, to decide on the appropriate treatment of single independent students, that treatment will be advantageous for all parents whose contribution would have been calculated to be greater than zero if their children were determined dependent. This means that the administrative criteria chosen must refer only to facts not easily falsified, simulated, or created *ad hoc* for the sake of advantageous treatment.

The recently revised rules for determining independence have not resolved the difficulties in a satisfactory way. By these rules a student is held to be dependent if:

1. The student has received more than $750 from parents in the last completed calendar year or expects to in the year for which aid is requested, or
2. The student has lived in the parents' home for more than six weeks in the last completed calendar year, or expects to do so in the year for which aid is requested, or
3. The student has been claimed as an exemption for federal income tax purposes in the last completed calendar year or expects to be in the one for which aid is requested

These rules attempt to assess the habitual nature of the dependence of children on parents. An investigation to verify either of the first two tests would be highly intrusive. Where parents and children are alienated, they might well resist verification of the third. The facts needed to satisfy the tests can be artificially created.

It is perhaps impossible to resolve all of the problems of constructing a widely acceptable set of administrative criteria for the independence of younger single students. One way of simplifying these problems is to determine independence for the purpose of student aid programs administered on a national or statewide basis by simple rules requiring only easy and relatively nonintrusive forms of verification. These rules should recognize the independence of single students only in the clearest cases— cases which are difficult to falsify and which could be created *ad hoc* only in ways that would tend to involve disadvantages outweighing any advantage. It would then be left to student aid officers to determine the validity of evidence rebutting the assumptions of these simple rules. They would, in effect, identify an additional class of independent students, including some "hard cases," "borderline cases," and cases where independence can be verified only by close examination of sensitive information supplied by students or parents. Additional student aid awarded by the student aid officer on the basis of such findings would be from discretionary student aid funds—from the colleges' allocations from the proposed Basic Grant set-aside and the SEOG program, or from institutional aid funds.

With this division of responsibility for determining independence, a set of criteria for programs administered nationally or statewide could be fairly simple. Those students might be determined independent for these programs if:

- They are over age 22 and have family responsibilities of their own, as evidenced by marriage and birth certificates
- They are over age 25, as evidenced by birth certificates
- They are orphans, as evidenced by death certificates
- They have been fully self-supporting for three consecutive years immediately preceding their aid applications, as evidenced by Internal Revenue Service documents showing earnings of $3,000 a year or more

The proportion of students applying for aid who apply as independent students has grown markedly in recent years under both the College Scholarship Service and Basic Grant systems for assessing parent and student contributions (Table 27). So has the proportion of students receiving aid as independent stu-

Table 27. Percentage of aid applicants claiming independent status

	Academic year	
	1974-1975	*1977-1978*
College Scholarship Service	10.9	23.4
Basic Grant system	19.5	38.3

dents (Section 6). Student aid officers report instances of families trying to take unintended advantage of the present rules. However, adequately verified statistical data is not available to establish the proportion of all students determined to be independent who, in some sense, should not be. A considerable growth has occurred in the number of older students and of students who have "stopped out" and entered the adult work force long enough for parental obligations to atrophy. At least a sizeable fraction of students of both kinds are properly eligible for aid as independent students by general consensus. There are also more students, both full- and part-time, whose identification should not be a major issue because they have assumed family responsibilities of their own. Further, there are those whose aim in establishing independence is not so much to take advantage of student grant programs but to meet the requirements for resident tuition subsidies in a state other than that where their parents live. Figures for all independent students tend to confound these categories, so data are not available to estimate the proportion of all independent students whose independence does not reflect the intentions of public policy but who gain such status because of the arbitrariness of the rules, abuse of the rules, mistakes in filling out forms, or perhaps merely the impulse to save the often considerable trouble of obtaining parental financial data.

The dependency status of low-income students deserves special discussion. Many families with incomes in, say, the lowest one fourth of all families simply cannot afford, or culturally do not acknowledge, the dependency of children over school-leaving age. It is probable that relatively few students from these families receive as much support from their parents as they do from their own earnings, unless they live at home. Of those who do live at home, some are net contributors to family finances. For these reasons, and because of the difficulty in many cases of obtaining financial data from parents, we should expect higher proportions of students from low-income families to apply for aid as independent students, and, as their numbers increase, to increase the proportion of all students who are independent. While none of these reasons for claiming independent status are necessarily sanctioned by the present rules on independence, they are not strongly at odds with them either. Certainly, abuse is not the issue, since the expected parental contribution of students from low-income families would normally be zero in any case, and there is, therefore, no financial advantage in being determined independent. If too many students are gaining by independent status, the problem is with students from middle- and upper-income families, not with those from low-income families.

Comparability of Treatment

Figure 26 illustrates the treatments suggested for various types of "nontraditional" students in comparison with that recommended for dependent full-time students.

Figure 26. Illustrative support toward noninstructional costs for lower-division students differing in enrollment and dependency status

Student category					
Full-time single dependent student	Standard self-help $600	Parental contribution $500	Basic Grant $1300		
Half-time single dependent student	Pro-rata standard self-help $300	Additional self-help $1200	Parental contribution $500	Basic Grant $400	
Full-time single independent student	Standard self-help $600	Basic Grant $1800			
Half-time single independent student	Pro-rata standard self-help $300	Additional self-help $1200	Basic Grant $900		
Full-time student with family responsibilities and loss of time for other activities, valued at $600.	Family contribution $500	Basic Grant $1300	Discretionary grant $600		
Half-time student with family responsibilities and loss of time for other activities, valued at $600.	Pro-rata standard self-help $300	Additional self-help $600	Family contribution $500	Basic Grant $400	Discretionary grant $600

Source: Carnegie Council Staff.

15

Enhancing Program Coordination

The importance of the goal of more equal educational opportunity in the growth of publicly financed student aid programs suggests that the various programs would have been designed to complement each other to this end and that their administrative mechanisms would have been coordinated. This, however, is far from the case. The programs were enacted at different times with different groups of beneficiaries most prominently in view. The programs have developed different constituencies and have recruited different advocates.

Moreover, the mixed public and private character of American higher education has posed a basic problem for an egalitarian student aid strategy: Should student aid have as its first priority to equalize "access," that is, to assure a chance for every young person to attend a low-priced, usually public, institution? Or should it provide, possibly at the expense of access programs, a more equal opportunity for "choice," that is, attendance at an expensive and often selective private institution? A multiplicity of programs, some with rules more favorable to access than choice, or vice versa, has permitted policy makers to compromise this difficult issue.

Still, it would be nearly unthinkable for major programs in such areas as welfare, unemployment compensation, or health insurance to operate without ground rules for coordination of benefits. One would expect a lack of clear complementarity among the student aid programs to be the source of endless trouble. It has indeed been. The fact that such a lack of system has been tolerable at all is due to the campus student aid officers, whose task it is to "package" aid from the various programs for which an individual student may be eligible. "Packaging" is itself a form of coordination.

Coordination by Packaging

When the present system works well it is because all the premises of the packaging process the student aid officer conducts turn out to be valid, both from the perspective of the individual student aided and in terms of the relative claims of other students. Some of these premises are consistently valid:

- Entitlement aid is generally reliable in amount, if not always in timing of receipt.
- Need analysis systems provide consistent information on the ability to pay of all families submitting accurate information.
- An inadequacy of aid funds under one program can readily be compensated by the use of funds under other programs, provided enough discretionary funds are available to the student aid officer.
- An aid officer is usually in a position to carry out a uniform policy for his or her institution concerning the amount of earning and borrowing expected of aided students.
- The aid officer has genuine discretion in estimating the needs and resources of students in the light of their special circumstances.
- The aid officer is in a position to adjust the amount of each type of support—grants, earnings, and borrowings—on the basis of the burdens the student can be expected to manage currently and in the future.

What is wrong with present program arrangements is reflected in limitations on the effectiveness and equity of the packaging process as a means of coordinating benefits:

- It is easy to find instances of *prima facie* unfairness in the

relative treatment of students, because program rules and
fund availabilities create anomalies among states, among colleges, and among students. Public faith in the system suffers
accordingly.

- Lack of any fundamental coordination reduces the benefit
  that can accrue from making any one program better and
  more simply administered; rather, it seems to impel efforts to
  complicate the individual programs to reduce inequities.
  Complexity then makes the programs vulnerable to abuse.
- The roles of parents and students themselves in financing education become more uncertain, and uncertainty gives rise to
  anxiety that financing for college will not be available. Each
  constituency and income class comes to feel that it must lock
  in "its share" of the benefits of student aid.

Moreover, the coordination of programs achieved by the
student aid officer has an after-the-fact character. The entitlement aid the student is eligible for (mainly, Basic Grants, veterans benefits, social security, and some state aid) must be
taken as a given by the aid officer. It may, in some cases, cover
all of a student's financial need; but, in other cases, little or
none. The aid officer must do the best he can to round off the
rough corners that result. He must rely on discretionary resources to try to increase the funds of students not favored by
the entitlement programs. Discretionary funds are scarce, and
the aid officer must try to conserve them as best he can by
sending as many students as possible off campus to find jobs
and loans, with little certainty that they will find them, although they are counted on in the students' aid packages.
Because of the inadequacy of state tuition grant programs in
most parts of the country, the rationing of available discretionary resources can be particularly desperate at many private
colleges.

Political Coordination

Improvement of this situation will require coordination before
the fact—a serious effort by the public programs to decide
about the kind and amount of need each program will be de-

signed to meet, and how the programs should fit together. It is hard to exaggerate how chaotic present statutory and regulatory coordination policies are. Federal law makes far more students eligible for aid, and in far larger amounts, than are ever expected to receive it. Amounts to be appropriated for different programs are related by historical formulas rather than by complementarity of mission. Need itself is differently defined for different programs. A student aid officer is routinely put in a position of estimating a Basic Grant using one set of figures for subsistence costs and then having to turn around and use quite another set for the campus-based federal programs. He estimates expected family contributions one way for Basic Grants, another way for the campus-based programs, and then disregards family contribution altogether in determining eligibility for a Guaranteed Student Loan. In some programs, aid is expected to be matched by other aid; but, in others, not.

These conflicting policies are not inadvertent. Each represents an attempt to favor students from one income bracket over others or to prefer students attending one type of institution over others. These preferences are intended to operate either by shifting the distribution of aid awards or by controlling the relative level of appropriations for different programs. Such rules represent an essentially political approach to coordination, in which each interest group fights hardest for the programs and program rules most favorable to the students it represents. A kind of balance and fairness certainly can result—the fairness of political compromise. But in the process the goal of creating a structure that will provide the most educational opportunity in the simplest, most economical way can easily be obscured or lost. And such an approach engenders strife among income groups and groups of institutions at least as often as it resolves conflict.

Getting from the present chaotic state of affairs to one in which coordination serves the broad goals of student aid will not be easy, but it is not impossible. First, we do not have to arrive at consensus about all the particulars of the system. Much better coordination could be achieved if we only had basic rules assigning roles in the system for parents, students, governments, and institutions and broad specifications for aid programs that would invoke or complement those roles. Second, the opposed positions on "access" and "choice" and on the relative claims of different income classes may not be so irreconcilable as they appear. There is a good chance that these competitive pressures would be much reduced if a coordinated student aid system held out the promise of simple and reliable arrangements for making the costs of higher education manageable for all students at all types of institutions. Good coordination can reduce conflict, rather than merely accommodate it. The kind of coordination we recommend would be based on principles of responsibility—principles that make sense in terms of the responsibilities governments, families, and students themselves should undertake.

Federal and State Responsibilities

Crucial to achieving better overall coordination is defining federal and state roles that would enable both federal and state authorities to avoid duplication of effort without risking a denial of adequate opportunities to students. Federal and state roles should be consistent with the larger distribution of responsibilities that has emerged in recent decades. The federal government increasingly has been seen as having special responsibilities:

- To promote equality of opportunity and to overcome obstacles to the enrollment of young people from low-income families and disadvantaged minority groups
- To support graduate education and research benefiting the nation as a whole
- To offset differences among the states in their fiscal capacity to support higher education

In connection with the first and third of these responsibilities, it is highly appropriate for the federal government to take the lead in providing aid that will assure that all students can meet the basic subsistence costs entailed by college attendance. This is an area states were late to enter, and they have entered very unevenly. It is an area where program criteria and mechanisms can be most properly uniform nationally, because, compared to the wide differences in typical tuition costs, subsistence costs vary relatively little among most states. It is, further, an area the federal government can enter with the least risk that its influence will intrude on institutional governance or tend to impose uniformity on educational programs. And it is an area where the federal government can be even-handed between public and private institutions.

At the same time, the states should be left with the primary role in matters related to the costs of instruction and the extent to which those costs are passed on to the student as tuition charges. It should be a matter primarily between a state and its citizens—whether students, parents of students, or non-students—how much public institutions will charge for tuition. The role of the state in student aid should be related to this determination, with decisions left to the state about the kind of student aid programs that will best enable students to meet tuition charges. Since the difference between tuition at public and private institutions is largely an artifact of state intervention to reduce public institution tuition, the state's role in student aid should also extend to aid programs that will narrow the "tuition gap" and support the participation of the institutions of the private sector in meeting the educational aspirations of the state's citizens. The federal role, in connection with what may be called "tuition sensitive" forms of student aid, should be supportive, not preemptive.

The division of responsibility suggested here will help preserve a viable form of federalism in the new circumstances of greater emphasis on equality of opportunity and on making the cost of college manageable for all. It will also have very practical value. Both federal and state student aid programs can be simpler, more efficient and more focused on specific sets of distinct problems.

Program Complementarity

What before-the-fact coordination requires, at a minimum, is a set of rules that say that eligibility for one program begins only where eligibility for others leaves off. And there needs to be an understood sequencing of programs and eligibilities that avoids Alphonse and Gaston situations.

We believe it would be sensible for entitlement grants, Basic Grants in particular, to come first. Following Basic Grants would be state grants and, after both, loans. With only this degree of coordination, it becomes possible to estimate financial need consistently and to gear both federal and state aid to differences in parental ability to pay for education, in keeping with equal opportunity objectives. The expected parental contribution would first reduce Basic Grant eligibility. Then, if the parental contribution is not exhausted by this reduction, any excess over the maximum amount of Basic Grant eligibility would be applied to reducing state grant eligibility.

It should be pointed out that if this kind of coordination is not worked out, there can be serious duplications of benefits. If, for example, federal and state programs proceed independently in reducing grants by the amount of expected parental contributions, these contributions will, in effect, be counted twice. Assuming federal and state programs with the same means test and the intent to meet the same levels of financial need, a student from a family with an expected family contribution $100 greater than that of another family will get $100 less from the federal program and $100 less from the state program also. Thus, aid will decline with higher levels of income more than expected parental contributions increase. Such situations have occurred in the past and, somewhat paradoxically, they are most likely to occur when the intent of federal and state programs is most similar and both are adequately funded.

Coordination and Self-Help Expectations

Besides helping to avoid situations such as that just described, the kind of coordination suggested also makes it possible to have a fair and consistent self-help expectation. Uniform self-help expectations can be introduced as an amount of expenses that neither federal or state grants are available to cover. Unless federal and state grant programs are coordinated in this way, a self-help expectation intended to be uniform will not be so in fact. If federal and state grants double-count expected parental contributions, the amount left for self-help after federal and state grants will vary from student to student (Figure 27).

Figure 27. Effect of double-counting parental contributions on implicit self-help contributions

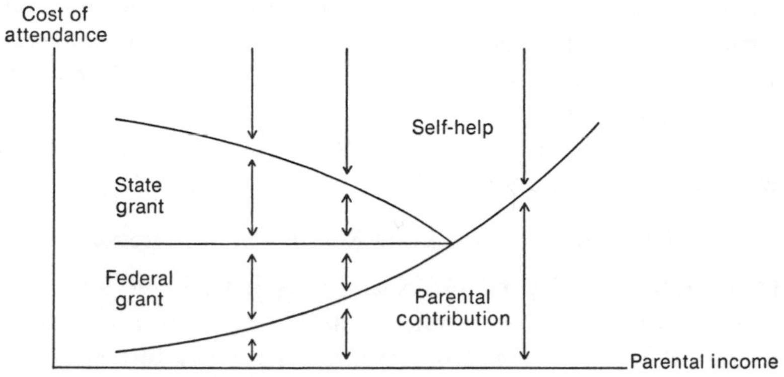

Coordination by Covering Specific Expenses

A second kind of program coordination, consistent with the first, is to have ground rules associating aid from each source with a specific type of college expense. In particular, it would be highly desirable to make the federal Basic Grant program the leading source of aid to enable students to meet subsistence expenses not covered from parental and personal resources and to make state scholarships the leading source of aid to meet tuition expenses beyond what the family can afford.

Proceeding in this way would greatly clarify federal and state roles. It would make it far easier for individual states to design programs and define eligibility for aid. A state would know, for example, that its grants would not be needed to meet noninstructional costs and that parental contributions in excess of such costs could be regarded as available to meet tuition charges. A state could concentrate its funds on meeting tuition expenses not covered by such parental resources. The federal government, for its part, could concentrate on providing a guarantee that all students could meet noninstructional costs.

In the past, it has not been possible for either a state or the federal government to rely with any confidence on the other's performance of an understood role. Uncertainty about the role and funding of the federal Basic Grant program has led some states to feel that they must also devote funds to subsistence grants. At the same time, the Congress has felt considerable concern that federal programs in which awards vary with tuition be continued, not being able to count on the states to deal with the need for tuition grants. The result has been the cases cited earlier where the sum of federal and state grants differ more between students in different family income brackets than expected family contributions differ for those brackets.

Federal Support for State Scholarship Programs

However, if equality of opportunity is a national goal—as it surely is—the federal government should support the states in the role described here. Differences between state tuition and student aid policies can be so extreme as to make the financing of tuition costs a very different matter for students in different states. Although decisions on such matters should be made at the state level, the federal government can appropriately provide financial incentives to bring states closer to providing adequate tuition grant programs.

Federal financial incentives are also needed to counter the natural tendency of the states to prefer students choosing home-state institutions. State student aid should not be awarded so much more favorably to students attending home-state institutions as to make going elsewhere a major and distinct financial obstacle in itself. In providing federal matching grants to encourage state spending for student aid, the federal formula should provide a special inducement for states to make their grants portable out-of-state, at least on a basis of reciprocity—that is, where another state also allows such portability.

The existing State Student Incentive Grant (SSIG) program provides an incentive for states to spend more on student aid, but this incentive is limited by the small size of federal appropriations for the program and by so-called maintenance-of-effort rules which require that most state expenditures before enactment of the federal program be disregarded in calculating a state's matching funds. The reforms suggested here call for larger federal appropriations and new rules on matching-grant calculations (Recommendations 9 and 11). Table 28 shows state-by-state estimates of federal and state matching funds for the proposed tuition grant program, in comparison with current state programs.

Sharing the Burden

Coordination along the lines suggested would involve a number of parties in the effort to overcome financial obstacles to higher education. Contributions by parents, students themselves, the federal government, and state governments are all indispensable. But there is an inevitable degree of complexity that results from such shared responsibility. It will perhaps be worthwhile to summarize "who does what" in the kind of overall system of student aid implied by these principles and reflected in Recommendations 1, 4, 11, and 16.

It is, of course, the task of federal and state governments to provide the fundamental ground rules for public programs. In extending and modifying the existing Basic Grant program, the Congress would need to define the level of noninstructional costs the program should guarantee that all students will be able to meet.

The parents' role would be to meet basic subsistence costs, if possible, and—if this is also possible—tuition costs. To supplement their resources, parents would look to the Basic Grant program to meet unaffordable minimum subsistence costs and would look first to state scholarship programs to meet unaffordable tuition costs. The federal government would provide incentives for states to mount grant programs on a scale that would provide grants to all students needing such assistance toward tuition expenses.

Obtaining aid under these arrangements could be a fairly simple matter if common means tests and common definitions of costs of attendance were adopted. Parents would need to fill out only one statement of their financial resources and send it to an agency that would, subject to verification, certify the

Table 28. Actual federal and state expenditures on state need-based grant programs, 1978-79, compared with estimated expenditures, 1982-83 (in 1979 dollars) under Carnegie Council proposals

	1978-79 actual			Estimated expenditures, 1982-83[b] (in 1979 dollars)		
	Federal	State	Total	Federal	State	Total
Alabama	$ 955	$ 1,216	$ 2,171	$ 15,630	$ 13,599	$ 29,299
Alaska	75	75	150	353	353	706
Arizona	750	750	1,500	7,065	6,181	13,246
Arkansas	374	373	747	5,934	5,122	11,038
California	11,700	71,873	83,573	65,170	64,110	129,281
Colorado	796	9,150	9,956	16,337	14,217	30,554
Connecticut	791	7,119	7,910	11,127	10,155	21,282
Delaware	173	368	541	3,356	2,914	6,270
District of Columbia	437	436	873	14,394	12,540	26,933
Florida	1,922	7,229	9,151	24,108	21,017	45,125
Georgia	1,111	2,064	3,175	16,867	14,659	31,525
Hawaii	248	248	496	1,236	1,060	2,296
Idaho	206	206	412	706	618	1,325
Illinois	3,371	80,904	84,275	30,201	41,859	92,058
Indiana	1,266	19,834	21,100	31,967	29,671	61,638
Iowa	677	12,864	13,541	14,482	15,764	28,246
Kansas	706	3,709	4,415	9,184	8,124	17,308
Kentucky	745	3,914	4,659	15,542	13,511	29,053
Louisiana	300	300	600	8,566	7,418	15,983
Maine	229	862	1,091	6,093	5,387	11,480

State					
Maryland	1,100	3,900	5,000	15,630	15,365	30,996
Massachusetts	2,178	13,379	15,557	43,182	38,707	81,948
Michigan	2,584	26,128	28,712	42,475	44,418	86,893
Minnesota	1,073	25,754	26,827	17,838	15,983	33,821
Mississippi	555	554	1,109	8,831	7,683	16,513
Missouri	1,227	7,538	8,765	22,253	19,427	41,681
Montana	176	175	351	2,296	2,031	4,327
Nebraska	420	420	840	8,389	7,329	15,719
Nevada	200	200	400	1,148	971	2,119
New Hampshire	250	250	500	8,742	7,683	16,425
New Jersey	1,822	34,626	36,448	17,220	22,077	39,296
New Mexico	300	,300	600	3,885	3,356	7,241
New York	5,286	259,014	264,300	91,221	114,445	205,666
North Carolina	1,371	1,370	2,741	24,726	21,547	46,273
North Dakota	165	178	343	1,766	1,501	3,267
Ohio	2,333	23,592	25,925	59,335	51,668	111,003
Oklahoma	1,437	1,436	1,873	9,360	8,124	17,485
Oregon	764	5,602	6,366	9,890	9,096	19,215
Pennsylvania	3,020	72,480	75,500	57,311	80,800	138,111
Rhode Island	331	2,974	3,305	9,890	9,537	19,427
South Carolina	800	9,194	9,994	10,420	9,096	19,516
South Dakota	133	132	265	4,504	3,885	8,389
Tennessee	1,020	3,230	4,250	22,606	19,692	42,299
Texas	3,382	11,992	15,374	24,726	21,547	46,273
Utah	465	1,393	1,858	5,210	4,592	9,802

(continued on next page)

Table 28 (continued)

	1978-79 actual			Estimated expenditures, 1982-83[b] (in 1979 dollars)		
	Federal	State	Total	Federal	State	Total
Vermont	$ 154	$ 3,701	$ 3,855	$ 7,241	$ 6,888	$ 14,129
Virginia	1,325	2,161	3,486	19,869	17,308	37,177
Washington	1,244	3,365	4,609	8,654	7,506	16,160
West Virginia	395	2,429	2,924	3,974	3,532	7,506
Wisconsin	1,385	21,700	23,085	20,752	19,869	40,621
Wyoming	55	140	195	883	795	1,678
Total	$63,825	$765,058[a]	$828,883	$917,000	$917,000[a]	$1,834,000

[a]The difference between these two totals does not represent the aggregate amount of proposed increases in state funding because some states would be able to reduce funding. The aggregate amount of all increases is $401 million.

[b]Estimates allow for difference among states' income levels and in enrollment patterns in public and private institutions, but they assume that the percentage of students migrating to other states is the same for each state (conforming to the national pattern).

Sources: National Association of State Scholarship and Grant Programs (1978) and Carnegie Council estimates.

amount of Basic Grant eligibility. If a relatively expensive college had been chosen, the parents could indicate the college on the form submitted and copies would be forwarded to the appropriate state scholarship agency. The state agency would notify the student and parents of the amount of the state grant for which the student was eligible. There would, of course, be controls on the disbursement of aid once the student actually enrolled and there would be special procedures for various categories of exceptional cases. But the great bulk of students and parents would know promptly what they could expect.

Part of what is at stake in achieving greater program coordination is such predictability. To the extent that agreement is reached about the roles to be played by the various sources of student finance, and to the extent that these roles become stable and well understood by students and parents, it will become possible to plan ahead on how college expenses will be met. The lack of predictability in the present largely uncoordinated system means that a student cannot put together a financial plan until he or she hears from the student aid officers of particular colleges—whose suggested plans may be strikingly different. This is surely a source of anxiety. It may work to limit the horizon of choice for many low-income students. It may also be a powerful component of the distress of middle-income families that takes the form of demands for tax relief. Tax relief would, at least, be predictable, although not, in fact, sensitively responsive to the variety of middle-income financial situations.

16

Increasing Integrity
and Simplicity

Student aid programs need to be fair and efficient in the way they are actually conducted as well as in intent. The public has a proper concern with questions about how student aid programs work:

- Do they get money to the right students in the right amounts to create the opportunities intended?
- Do the students who receive aid in fact use it to obtain such opportunities?
- Are the programs protected from those who want to manipulate them for other ends?
- Are the programs realistic and economical in their demands on the time and effort of students, parents, and administrators?

There is probably no one who would now answer with an unqualified "yes" to any of the above questions. There have been too many anecdotes about students who get too much or too little aid, or whose aid awards are substantial and whose enrollments are nominal. There have been too many newspaper accounts of fraud against students and the government in the student loan programs.

It is not as though efforts were not being made to guard the integrity of the programs. Student aid applications are checked for inconsistency by computer and by hand. Regulations spell out in elaborate detail just what procedures must be carried out in the awarding of aid. The disbursement of funds is also elaborately regulated. Auditors examine the records of institutions with some frequency, especially if problems have been uncovered in the past. In fact, a bureaucracy has developed that is large by almost any standard and that has a responsibility as much to prevent and correct abuse as to deliver aid to needy students. Those who do not have to deal with this bureaucracy or have need to deal with only one part of it are probably unaware of its size because it is so decentralized. It consists of federal administrators in Washington and in federal regional offices, of large nonprofit organizations which administer means test systems, of loan officers and collection agents in banks and other credit institutions, of state loan and scholarship agencies, and, of course, of student aid offices and business offices on every campus. Administering the student aid system probably provides the equivalent of full-time employment for 15,000 to 20,000 people.

It is difficult to assess in the aggregate the problems of student aid abuse that have resisted the efforts of all of these people. At the aggregate level, much depends on how *abuse* is defined. Only recently, for example, a redefinition of the term *default* as applied to the National Direct Student Loan program has, overnight, changed perceptions of that program, so that instead of being viewed as an endeavor almost beyond reproach, it is now regarded as one in very serious difficulty. Equally definitional is the question of whether it is an abuse not to repay a grant that was understood to be outright but was not, in fact, used in accordance with regulations. Does nonrepayment count as an abuse in addition to the infraction of the regulations? Other ambiguities are conceptual rather than technically definitional. For example, in some cases, efforts to collect loans have been so nearly nonexistent that blaming a student for delinquency in repayment is rather like blaming a castaway on a desert island for not getting to church on Sunday. Again, the opportunities for taking undue advantage of the programs have often been so broad that deciding which are cases of culpable abuse and which are not is rather like deciding which of several people given free access to a well-stocked larder took possession of food wrongly because they were greedy or took possession rightly because they were hungry. A common-sense, let alone statistical, appraisal of the overall problem of abuse in the student aid programs appears simply impossible.

Whatever the actual level of abuse, it is intolerable to have a student aid system that so often seems to invite it. It is also intolerable to have a system that is so complicated that credibility of purpose is lost. Vulnerability to abuse and excessive complexity are closely related. If the rules are too complicated for anyone to assess their implications in combination, the probability is high that they will interact in particular circumstances to create an unforeseen opportunity for abuse. In any case, the number of technical and venial infractions will multiply, and this may easily swamp and distract efforts to deal with seriously unethical behavior.

Accordingly, proposed improvements in the way the student aid programs operate should meet a double test. Any set of proposals for reducing the vulnerability of the programs to abuse should not only pass the test of effectiveness in that respect but should also be shown likely to reduce complexity. On the other hand, any approach to simplifying the programs should also meet the test of reducing invitations to abuse.

This sounds complicated, and it is. A properly strong concern for greater program integrity can easily lead to a wish to take simple and direct corrective action. Unfortunately, however, preventing abuse and simplifying the programs is itself a far from simple matter. They require that we take into account a set of paradoxes:

- Although we feel moral outrage at many kinds of abuse, the prevention of abuse is usually a matter of cool-headed management.
- The analysis required to frame good, simple rules may be complex; the analysis behind complex rules may be all too simple.
- A program's vulnerability to abuse need not necessarily be

dealt with in that program. Sometimes the source of the problem can be shifted to another program and corrected more effectively there.

- Hard cases make bad law. In particular, rules designed to give special help to the especially deserving lead people to try to establish that they are so deserving and this forces administrators to decide between such claims on poor and easily falsified information.
- The more conditions we impose on the receipt of aid, even in the interest of program integrity, the harder it is to maintain that integrity, because there are more rules whose circumvention must be guarded against.
- The public interest in the proper use of student aid funds is often best protected if students are convinced that it is their own money, not public money, that is at risk.
- The burden of compliance with rules designed to prevent abuse falls most heavily on honest individuals, who make the greatest effort to comply, not on those whose intention is to take unethical advantage of the system.

In addition to these apparent contradictions, a number of difficult trade-offs are involved in an effort to reduce abuse and complexity. A fundamental source of complexity in student aid programs is a wish to channel aid to students (or to institutions for redistribution to students) in amounts just sufficient to meet their needs. This requires collecting information pertinent to need analysis and attaching eligibility for aid to such characteristics. Efficiency, in one sense, requires that this be done, because aid available without such conditions would have to be distributed in the same amounts to students with or without need. Obviously, such an unconditional program would cost more to assure any given level of opportunity than one in which only the needy received aid. But, at some point, such a system for rationing aid becomes so complex as to be inefficient in another sense. The demands it makes on individuals to provide information, the demands it places on administrators to check and use that information, and the multiplication of occasions for abuse all tend to reduce efficiency. We must be prepared at some point to weigh the one kind of inefficiency against the other, and also to assign weight to the moral hazard of putting unscrupulous people at an advantage over the scrupulous. Ultimately, we must be prepared to find that somewhat less efficiency through the rationing of aid would be preferable to greater but perhaps spurious precision in the rationing system. The same goes for finer distinctions of equity: we must be prepared to find at some point that proliferation of distinct treatments of students in slightly different situations might be more equitable in principle, but less equitable in practice, if it also entails the proliferation of opportunities for abuse and reduced administrative effectiveness.

To take into account the paradoxes and trade-off judgments involved, an effort to simplify and reduce the vulnerability of student aid programs needs to be fairly orderly and comprehensive. Figure 28 suggests such an approach. Each cell indicates a problem area; the cross-hatched and dark-bordered areas indicate similarities among problems.

A first principle—and a first set of steps to take—is to eliminate, wherever possible, unnecessary procedures that constitute occasions for abuse. Scattered over Figure 28 are a number of cross-hatched cells indicating the following cases where abuse frequently occurs in carrying out a procedure that is probably unnecessary:

1. The allocation of Basic Grant funds to institutions is by way of advances to cover the estimated number of vouchers each institution expects to have presented over a particular calendar period. Use of estimates offers a modest opportunity for an institution to obtain interest-free credit for a short period. Such abuses are relatively minor in importance, but could be eliminated almost entirely by calculating advances as a percentage of vouchers actually presented a year earlier, rather than by using estimates.

2. The eligibility of a student to borrow under the NDSL program is now established only through a test of the family's ability to pay. Such tests make sense because of the large

Figure 28. Potential for abuse by program and transaction

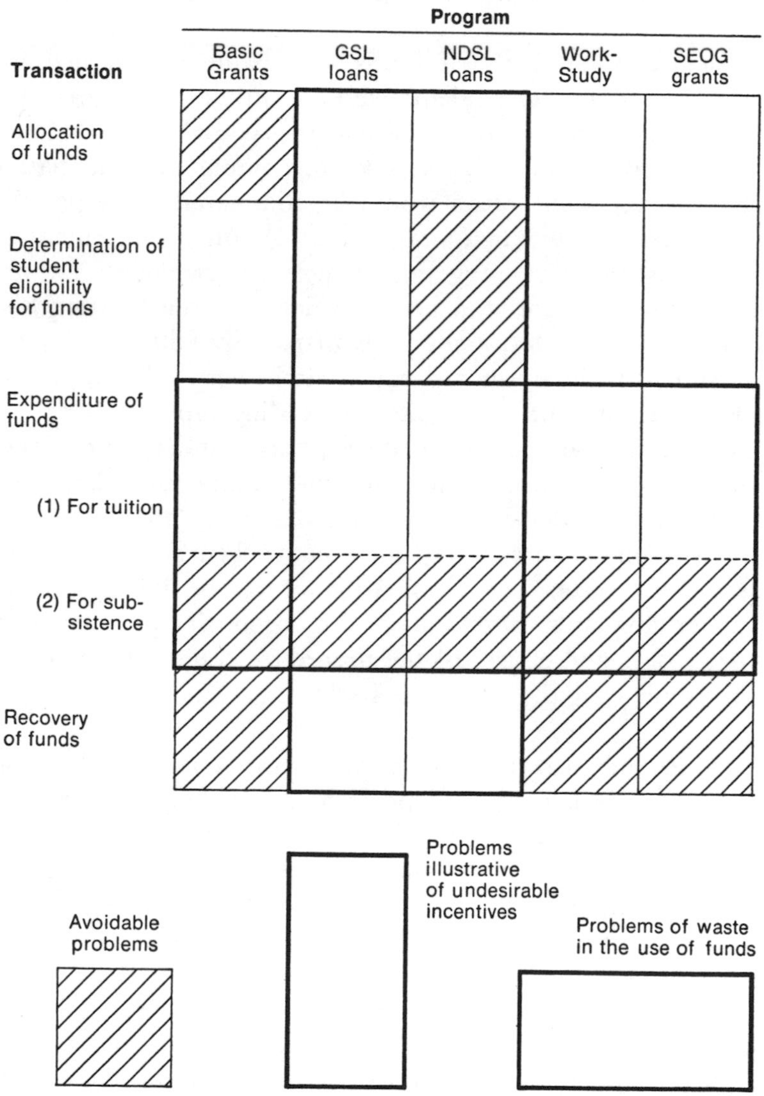

interest subsidies—in effect grants—provided by the program. If the subsidies were eliminated or made repayable with interest, there would be no need for such tests. If additional means-tested aid is required, it could be provided grant programs, rather than through interest subsidies—through shifting the problem to programs where it can be dealt with more effectively.

3. The use of student aid funds to provide subsistence and pocket money for students who are not actively participating in course work, if at all, is a major type of abuse. If funds were paid out only on evidence of completed participation in courses, such abuses would be eliminated. An especially important candidate for such controls on disbursement of funds is the GSL program, because disbursements are not controlled by the student aid officer. A rule limiting borrowing to a modest amount—perhaps only $500—during the first half of the freshman year would be very helpful.

4. To deal with the immediately preceding type of abuse, the federal programs have issued regulations under which funds not used to support active participation in courses become a debt to the federal government owed by the student and his institution. Failure to pay these debts then becomes itself a separate abuse. The elimination of opportunities for the underlying abuse would make this accounting procedure unnecessary, and abuses of the procedure could be eliminated by eliminating the procedure itself.

A second principle is that incentives to perform desirable actions and disincentives to perform undesirable ones can reduce both complexity and vulnerability to abuse. There are a great many illustrations of this principle—or rather, its contravention—in the problems of the student loan programs, grouped together in the vertical column enclosed by a darker line in Figure 28. The case has previously been made for the creation of a National Student Loan Bank that could deal with many problems of overcomplexity and abuse at the same time it assured a reliable flow of loan funds to all who need them. In particular, a National Student Loan Bank would avoid the inevitable degree of complexity in any system, such as the current GSL program, that attempts to have private lenders adopt sound loan origination and servicing practices without giving them the usual incentives to do so—because of a justifiable fear that such incentives would also be incentives to screen loan applicants for credit worthiness. A National Student Loan Bank would also resolve the current problem of loan collections by using the federal income tax system to assure repayment. However, there are object lessons in the present GSL system that are worth reviewing, even if that system ought to be replaced entirely:

1. Adequate incentives for commercial providers of credit to supply funds for student loans have been lacking for much of the history of the GSL program. The permitted rate of return on student loans has reacted only sluggishly to changes in lender costs of money and costs of compliance with a changing and increasingly elaborate set of regulations. This has deterred regular commercial lenders from providing an adequate volume of loans. Consequently, the share of all loans made by lenders positioned to profit from the tuition payments financed by loans, as well as from interest yield, tended to grow until problems with this latter group of lenders forced regulatory and other curtailment of their participation. If a National Student Loan Bank is not established and if reliance upon private credit sources is continued, rates of return should be maintained at levels sufficient to give ordinary commercial lenders incentives to provide an adequate volume of loans. If this is done it would be less necessary—perhaps wholly unnecessary—to regulate in detail the kinds of transactions that educational institutions can engage in as lenders or with other parties who act as lenders.

2. There are now strong incentives for students not to play the part assigned to them in providing information on which the system depends. They are required by regulation to notify lenders when they discontinue their educational programs. Their "reward" is to have a 7 percent interest subsidy

benefit withdrawn and to be required to start making repayments. The kind of behavior demanded is too much to expect
even of relatively honest and well-meaning borrowers, let
alone of those who calculate their own advantage with fewer
scruples. However honest initially, students who become delinquent in these circumstances may come to make a habit
of it. Penalties are probably not the answer, for we probably
do not really want to apply penalties with a reasonable
amount of due process to enormous numbers of borrowers
whose delays in reporting can have any number of plausible
excuses. Rather, some part of the subsidy benefits of the
program (if continued at all) could be made contingent on
timely reporting and made to serve as an incentive to do so.
Again, some system for determining the period of subsidy
and the beginning of repayment obligations might be established that does not depend at all on a voluntary act of the
borrower.

A third principle is illustrated by the complexities and
abuse inherent in systems for determining the student's eligibility for aid: subtlety in distinguishing the differing claims of students for aid through means tests must not be allowed to
outrun practical and acceptable means of verifying those claims.
It was pointed out earlier that in a loan program where the student pays the true cost of borrowing it may be possible to avoid
the attempt to distinguish eligibility claims altogether. One can
imagine job programs with a wage so low that no one would
want one of the jobs provided except as a last resort. It would
therefore be unnecessary to have a means-test system for establishing eligibility for such jobs or any requirement for proof
that other jobs had been sought. But in grant programs some
mechanism to determine ability to pay and residual need is
needed.

On at least two points, the policy impulse to distinguish
relative equities in grant programs has gone beyond what can
reasonably be implemented. One is the problem of the "independent student"—the student whose parents are not expected
to contribute to college expenses. Many of these are students

from low-income families, whose independence may express the fact that the parents simply cannot provide support. But it is financially advantageous for other families if they can establish that no support is expected because a child is independent. As a consequence, any criterion for determining which students are independent must be readily verifiable and, more, must be such that parents and children cannot create in their own interest the set of facts that verify satisfaction of that criterion. Otherwise, the strongest incentives will operate to increase the number claiming and obtaining independent student status.

It would be easy enough to build workable criteria for independence on facts of record such as the student's age, income, and marital status (see Section 13). But there has been a tendency, instead, to search for sociological criteria that would somehow test the degree of alienation or attenuation in the relationship between children and parents and to look at, for example, housing arrangements and the kinds of material support recently provided or not provided. Undoubtedly, there are important changes occurring in family relationships, but it is surely a mistake to try to catch them in mid-evolution and to build an administrative apparatus on the variables of the moment.

Another instance of this third principle is the treatment of parental assets in means tests. Parents who are expected to provide the support they can are asked to report their assets as well as their incomes, and they are expected to make available a small fraction of their assets (net of debts) to meet educational expenses. But whereas many types of income are currently verifiable at their source, we have no routine way of appraising the value of assets. When appraisals are carried out—for example, at death or in the course of a divorce settlement—the complexities can be excruciating. The asset contribution in student aid eligibility systems is thus an assessment of a very rough kind. Conscientious parents who report all their assets are still guessing about values. Other parents find it easy to assign low values. To avoid unadministerable complexity and to reduce temptations to abuse, it may be preferable to ignore assets as such and to make a few—hopefully very few—adjustments to the contribution from incomes, such as providing a deduction for housing rent paid.

However, there is another way to resolve the dilemma that exists between the need to keep rules simple and the need to deal sensitively with the variability of human circumstance. As proposed in Recommendation 15, it is to have very simple rules, uniformly applied, when a state or federal agency must make a determination relating to need, and then to entrust enough funds to the student aid officer at the individual student's college so that he or she can allow for exceptions by awards of extra aid. Student aid officers should be accountable for such discretionary funds only to the extent of assuring that they have been applied to student aid purposes broadly defined. Under the recommendations we make, the student aid officer would have three main sources of such funds:

1. The Supplemental Educational Opportunity Grant (SEOG) program
2. An allocation from a special set-aside equal to 10 percent of the Basic Grant funds needed to meet uniform entitlements
3. The institution's own aid funds, including those released from routine use by the increasing adequacy of federal and state grant programs

A fourth principle is that a premium should not be placed on facile cleverness in obtaining funds. It is not, after all, the goal of the student aid programs to reward the particular intellectual skills involved in figuring out how to beat the system. Failure to observe this fourth principle is one of the factors that has led to several of the problems already reviewed. However, the clearest case of such failure is probably the system for allocating to particular colleges each state's allotments under the NDSL, Work-Study, and SEOG programs. The basic procedure in effect up to the fall of 1976 was for each institution to submit an application providing a forecast of the characteristics of its prospective student body that would permit a forward estimate of the aggregate financial need of its students. For this purpose, the institution's student aid officer projected numbers of students, costs of attendance, ability of students to pay, and student aid funds available from sources other than the three programs. These figures were then used to project the aggregate need of the student body. The vulnerability of this system was its dependence on forecast rather than actual data. An astute student aid officer knew how to be plausibly optimistic about enrollments and plausibly pessimistic about costs of attendance and the ability of families to pay and thereby inflate the aggregate need of the institution. The aid officer could thereby increase the institution's share of the funding requests that would be approved for the state. Funds actually available to institutions in the state were then distributed according to their shares of all approved requests. One institution's request inflated by plausible optimism and pessimism in forecasting thus reduced the final allocations of other institutions less well served by the cleverness of their student aid officers.

The results of this system for academic year 1977-78 seemed unreasonable to a large number of student aid officers and it appears to have been abandoned by the Office of Education. A current controversy concerns the kind of system that will replace it. To avoid a new invitation to competitive grantsmanship it would seem desirable to have an allocation method that would rely exclusively on institutional statistics, excluding forecasts, that can be verified at the time of application. Current Office of Education thinking appears to take this same view.

A fifth and final principle was mentioned earlier as a paradox: some abuses in the use of student aid funds can best be avoided if students are convinced that it is their own funds that are at risk, even if the funds come from public sources. This principle has application in the difficult area of trying to avoid waste and diversion in the spending of funds—the horizontal row enclosed by a dark outline in Figure 28. Part of the problem—the spending of funds for subsistence when the student is not actually using the time afforded to get on with an educational program—could be dealt with, as pointed out before, by delaying the disbursement of funds pending evidence that the student has actually participated in the program in which he or she has enrolled. But there is also a proper concern that the portion of student aid funds spent on tuition and fees should be well spent. An attempt by public authorities to review and certify the value of individual educational programs would run immense risks of bureaucratic error and incompetence, not to speak of interference in areas of proper academic freedom. The only slightly less direct approach of excluding all programs in a category where abuse has been relatively frequent—for example, all proprietary schools or all correspondence schools—would be heavy-handed, would be unfair to a great many worthwhile programs and would restrict the scope of student opportunities.

In the long run, the best assurance that students will get what their student aid pays for is to increase their awareness that what is wasted in paying for an inadequate program is their own money—an entitlement to grant aid that is being drawn down, earnings that represent their own efforts and money from loans that will assuredly have to be repaid. To reinforce the sense that student aid funds belong to the students themselves and to reactivate a sense of *caveat emptor,* it would help to let students "bank" their grant entitlements for use later in life, to charge realistic interest rates on student loans, and to assure that Work-Study jobs demand as much effort as jobs elsewhere in the economy (as they often, but not always, do). If students are then provided with the information they need as investors in educational programs, we will have perhaps the best protection that we can devise against erosion of the value of educational opportunities purchased through student aid.

17

Calculating
the Necessary Costs
of an Adequate System

The steps that now need to be taken to achieve an adequate student aid system are unlike those that were taken in the late 1960s and in the landmark federal legislation of 1972. Then the issue was to establish the principle that student aid, distributed on the basis of need, should assure every qualified student a chance to go to college. That principle was established, however tentatively, through enactment of a Basic Grant program with entitlement features.

However, in making this important breakthrough, the Congress did not articulate a comprehensive student aid system. Roles for student earnings, for loans, for state grants, and for campus-based discretionary programs were acknowledged, and, as it were, reserved. But principles for coordinating these roles were only sketched and administrators were left with the task of trying to find ways for the programs to work together with equitable results for individual students.

The issue now is how best to combine the elements of an aid system we have into a structure that meets these needs for coordination and equity. There is also a need that such structural questions be resolved in ways that protect the system against abuse and assure the public that its funds are being spent to help students who are making serious efforts to contribute to their own support.

In this new context, the aggregate dollar level of the public commitment to student assistance should be much less of an issue. The very rapid growth of funding for the Basic Grant program, the unintended growth of student loan subsidy and default costs, and increases in state funding have brought the cost of continuing programs now in existence to levels that few would have predicted five years ago. The overlap of social security student benefits and food stamps benefits with Basic Grants suggests that these resources can be freed for reallocation. We may be within reach of having an adequate set of student aid programs without having to commit relatively large increments of public resources to the system taken as a whole.

Of course, whether current levels of public funding are roughly adequate to meeting student need depends on how need is assessed. Differing need analysis systems lead to quite different estimates of aggregate student need. Table 29 shows alternative calculations of net aggregate need according to various means-test systems adjusted to take account of the impact of inflation on both incomes and family living expenses.

The best way to appraise these figures is to think of the "remaining need" figure shown as the upper limit to the amount students might need to borrow to meet college expenses if they and their parents cannot contribute more from current income and savings. If some of the more demanding means tests were entirely valid, there would, in principle, be ways of redistributing current aid funds to eliminate the need to borrow almost entirely, because parents would be providing a larger share of financing from private resources. On the other hand, estimating need for aid in the way that results in the greatest aggregate need—the current CSS/ACT method—suggests that borrowing might be substantial.

One can then ask whether it would be undesirable for a large share of this remaining need to be met by borrowing. In making a judgment on this issue, it should be kept in mind that much of such borrowing would be to relieve parents of burdens that in earlier years they would have been expected to bear and

Table 29. Projected aggregate student need and resources 1979-80—undergraduate students enrolled half-time or more (billions of 1979 dollars)

	Means-test system				
	CSS 1967-68	CSS 1973-74	CSS/ACT 1978-79	Basic Grants pre-1979	Basic Grants post-1979[b] (MISAA)
Aggregate expenses less expected parental contributions	15.0	15.5	18.2	9.2	17.2
Deduct: Aggregate student earnings of students whose expenses are not covered by parental contributions assessed by applicable means test[a]	6.2	5.8	6.9	3.9	8.1
Aggregate need before aid	8.8	9.7	11.3	5.3	9.1
Deduct:					
Projected federal and state aid funds, existing programs[c]	7.0	7.0	7.0	7.0	7.0
Projected private grant aid	1.4	1.4	1.4	1.4	1.4
Remaining need to be met from loans, savings, additional earnings, or additional parental contributions	.4	1.3	2.9	0	.7

[a]Calculated from 1975-76 average actual earnings according to Carnegie student survey, adjusted by percentage increase in federal minimum wage. Does not include additional self-help proposed in this report.

[b]As modified by the Middle-Income Student Assistance Act.

[c]Excludes G.I. Bill; includes food stamps.

Source: Carnegie Council staff estimates.

might try to bear now to reduce their children's indebtedness. Also, most of it would go toward financing the choice of high-cost institutions where lower-cost institutions were accessible. With creation of an NSLB, students could manage larger debt. If, holding these factors in mind, the amount of remaining need does not seem too high to be met in substantial part by borrowing, we can say that currently available student aid resources are roughly equal to the task of providing adequate student support. If the amount does seem too high, then the question recurs of whether mainly middle-income parents should dig somewhat deeper than the means tests expect or whether additional public funding should be provided to bring down the aggregate amount of potential student borrowing and, thus, to relieve students as well as their parents of financial burdens.

In our view, the CSS/ACT need analysis system is the best means test now in use. Its exemptions of income needed for the maintenance of other members of a family that is expected to contribute to a student's expenses are the most adequate, and make the system more progressive than the new Basic Grant system for families in the lower-middle-income range. Its expected rates of contribution increase appropriately with income, reinforcing the progressivity of the system over the upper-middle- and upper-income ranges. For these reasons, the system should be adopted for all federal and state grant programs.

But while the current CSS/ACT system results in the largest estimate of remaining financial need shown in Table 29, it does not suggest an amount of need, net of current levels of public and private aid, that would result in excessive student borrowing. Some parents would undoubtedly choose to contribute more than the CSS/ACT system expects. Many students could contribute more from earnings. Most of the borrowing that would occur would go toward financing choice.

We conclude that public funds for student aid at roughly current levels are adequate, when associated with the CSS/ACT standards, to assure that student need is met if distributed through a fair and coordinated aid system.

18

Assuring Commitment to the Most Essential Goals of Student Assistance

The present system of student aid for undergraduates satisfies almost no one. In part, this is because it is really a multitude of complicated systems attempting to serve many interests. Its complexity means that much can go wrong or can appear to go wrong. The complexity is itself the result of the still incomplete evolution of the goals of the student aid system over the last two decades. The trend of this evolution has been in the direction of a national commitment to equality of educational opportunity, but the nation has not yet fully articulated a set of programs that make such a commitment fully operational. At no point has the nation made a standing offer to its citizens that they could, on reasonable financial terms, attend any of a reasonable array of colleges to which they might be admitted. The federal legislation of 1972 took steps in this direction but held back from making a commitment to adequate program arrangements or funding. The programs we have represent accretions prefatory to such a commitment rather than such a commitment itself. We believe that such a commitment now will show the way toward a simpler, more stable, and more obviously fair system.

The Essential Commitments

Such a commitment would recognize that:

- An opportunity to go to college is, for all those qualified and motivated to do so, a critical opportunity for a productive, autonomous and socially responsible life.
- The full development of the intellectual capacities of our people, whether of great or modest talents, is vital to our future as a nation.
- Equality of opportunity for higher education is an indispensable part of any broader agenda for achieving equal opportunity in our society.

Those who would lower the relative priority of opportunity for higher education must be greatly underestimating the difficulties of living productively in our society without a level of education that, a few decades ago, might have seemed largely a luxury. It is not a luxury now. There are other pressing economic and social priorities, but it is precisely in order to enable the individual to deal with them responsibly as a citizen and as a private person that educational opportunities beyond high school are increasingly indispensable for many. Higher education opens to the individual a rich set of alternatives for intellectual and personal development. Without higher education—the skills it imparts and the credentials it confers—many of the careers and social roles important in a complex modern society are closed to the individual. There are other careers and roles that do not require education beyond high school, and our society has often failed to reward them and recognize their equality of status. But even if other avenues of opportunity were more open than they now are, we would still need to assure equality of opportunity for higher education to achieve basic social purposes.

These social purposes extend well beyond benefits to the individuals who take advantage of educational opportunities. Their families, their communities, and the nation as a whole benefit from being able to count on the greater competence and adaptability of those who have made good use of higher education opportunities. A wider range of choice in organizing to achieve group and national goals becomes possible. There is, moreover, what is perhaps the greatest public benefit of equality of opportunity: the shared knowledge that we are creating a society in which personal achievement is not limited by class or status but depends, in the main, on individual aspiration and performance.

The Conditions of Meeting These Essential Commitments

It is well, however, to attempt some precision in stating what equal opportunity for higher education entails. What are, and are not, necessary conditions of such equality have an important bearing on the adequacy of alternative student aid systems.

- *Who should have such opportunities?* The least restrictive definition would seem the best: All those who are qualified for admission and wish to attend college should be financially able to do so without regard to community, family and ethnic affiliations, or their private financial means.
- *What kinds of institutions should they be able to attend?* Avoidance of restriction would seem to entail that most institutions should be financially accessible to students meeting their admissions standards, excluding no numerous class of institutions. There may be some few institutions that are so expensive that an adequate general plan for enabling students to manage college costs would not cover all that these institutions charge. However, it would undercut equality of opportunity if, say, students were barred from attending a large proportion of private or highly selective institutions for financial reasons, even though they were enabled to go to college elsewhere.
- *How much financial support should students be eligible for?* A reasonable standard might be that the student aid system should provide enough support to overcome financial obstacles but not so much as to induce educationally irrelevant behavior. It should, on this standard, assure enough support so that all motivated students will be able to attend college without hardship, but it need not be enough to attract students without strong educational motivation.
- *What should be expected of students themselves and of their*

families? The previous points suggest that student aid should make financing the costs of higher education manageable for all. But a student aid system that succeeded in doing so need not go so far as to eliminate the need for sacrifice, effort, and commitment on the part of the student and the student's family. For younger and dependent students, a student aid system that compensated for differences in parental ability to pay for the college expenses students themselves could not meet would seem to define appropriate student, parental, and public roles. In such a system, adequate funds would be forthcoming, yet the commitment of parental resources and of students' own earnings and credit would give assurance that their participation is for serious educational purposes.

A student aid system meeting these broad specifications would do what student aid can and should do to contribute to equality of opportunity for higher education. Most clearly, it could enable disadvantaged students to overcome the obvious obstacle of a lack of money to meet college costs. It could also lend psychological support to college aspirations before students finish high school. Awareness of the adequacy and reliability of student aid could support motivation for college prerequisite courses. It could reinforce a realistic optimism about college prospects on the part of both students and their parents, and it could help ward off defeatism. Finally, if the student aid system permitted a reasonable choice among differing educational programs carrying different price tags, it could help a student choose an appropriate program, reducing the risks of disillusionment or failure. Too often, the differences between the costs of attending various colleges loom larger than they should in student choices, real as the differences are. They become too often a reason for not even considering promising alternatives. A stable and adequate student aid system would not only deal with real financial problems; it would also enable students and their parents to see those problems in a less restrictive perspective. But even though student aid can make all of these contributions to equality of opportunity, an adequate student aid system is not a sufficient condition of achieving such equality. The curriculum, the pedagogy that supports it, and all the aspects of the college environment that motivate or inhibit motivation can affect differently those of different backgrounds and cultures. Improvements in these areas should be sought independently of efforts to improve the student aid system and should be funded on their merits.

Nor can the measure of the success of the system be whether all groups in fact participate equally in higher education. In a society in which both values and aspirations differ, and in which college attendance is not compulsory, there will be different rates and patterns of attendance. In a society that respects personal and tentative choice, there will be many who do not choose college, who choose to postpone it, or who do not choose to continue beyond a self-determined point. For example, a sizeable proportion (about 15 percent) of those who have had traditionally the best opportunities for college—high-ability white males from upper-income families—do not choose to go to college. What should be achieved is a situation in which not going to college represents a genuine choice in all cases, because none would be forced not to attend college by their financial circumstances.

At the same time, highly unequal rates of college entrance must be suspect. If students from families of different incomes have widely differing rates of college entrance, regardless of similar abilities and aspirations, there is bound to be a suspicion that inequality of family resources is playing a role, either direct or indirect, in deterring the choice of additional education. Where rates of entrance differ widely for high-ability students from different income groups, the existence of equality of opportunity must especially be doubted. A developed taste for intellectual topics is usually associated with demonstrated high ability, and surely the brightest students are aware of the personal rewards of pursuing additional education. It would, therefore, be hard to believe that differing tastes and cultural backgrounds could account for a sizeable difference in college-going rates among very able students.

Figure 29 shows the rates of college entry that might be

Figure 29. College entrance rates by socioeconomic status and academic ability.
Actual percentage rates of high school graduates entering college 1961 and 1972, with 1985 rates
projected to result from adequate student aid programs

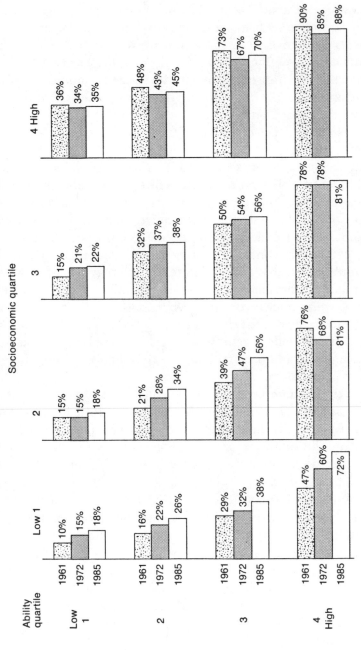

Sources: Adapted from Peng (1977) and The Carnegie Foundation for the Advancement of Teaching.

expected to result by 1985 from programs implementing the goal of equality of opportunity in the ways we recommend, in line with the earlier universal access projections of The Carnegie Foundation for the Advancement of Teaching (1975, Section 7.)

The Necessary Burdens

The standard for an adequate student aid system outlined here assumes that student aid should continue its primary role as a supplement to parental resources and the student's own self-help. The part student aid plays in financing higher education should grow until it performs this role of supplementation adequately. But this does not mean it should keep on growing beyond this and shift all of the burden of financing higher education from students and their families to the public. On the contrary, in the very long view, economic growth can be expected to allow parental contributions and student self-help to cover a rising proportion of higher education costs. Higher rates of real income will enable parents and students to pay more from current earnings and will also enable students to manage higher levels of indebtedness when they must borrow to meet costs in excess of current resources. Such development will be all to the good, bringing opportunities for higher education more and more within the realm of individual decisions about the use of personal resources, as they already are for many adult and part-time students.

We do not believe, however, that the contribution of students and their parents can yet relieve the public of its share of the financial burdens. Our criteria for an adequate student aid system incorporate the premise that for the next decade, at least, parents, students, and the public will all need to play their roles if equal opportunity objectives are to be realized. Many unavoidable complexities in the structure of student aid programs result from the need for mechanisms to apportion these responsibilities or to make them easier to carry out. To have an adequate student aid system, public policy will have to be prepared to deal with these minimum complexities, while avoiding any tendency to multiply them without necessity.

Reconciling Other Goals

As urgent as the equal opportunity goal of student aid programs is, it does not invalidate other goals for higher education. Among these are educational excellence, institutional health, and a manner of public intervention consistent with the best traditions of good government. Our recommendations have been framed with a view to these other goals along with the goal of equal opportunity. The purposes of student aid programs could be (and at times, perhaps, have been) pursued in ways that conflict with these other goals, but we do not believe they need be.

For example, it is sometimes argued that the equal opportunity emphasis in student aid programs has reduced the prestige of academic excellence and the material motivation to achieve it. If that is so, prizes and honors carrying cash value may be useful. However, we do not believe that such awards need divert efforts to establish a more general student aid system that attempts to provide aid on the basis of objective criteria of financial need.

A second aspect of the quality issue is a concern that students should receive aid in ways that strengthen and do not weaken the maturational side of education—what used to be thought of as its character-building purposes. It is often said that student aid has become a form of welfare—in the unfortunately pejorative sense of an unearned gain from a system that is to be beaten rather than participated in responsibly. We do not believe that student aid—any more than the welfare system—need conform to this stereotype. Simplification of the system, with due regard for the distortion of motivation that may result from naively framed formulas and mechanisms, can avoid these hazards.

The student aid system can, in fact, help define situations for individual students that will make a positive contribution to their personal maturation. This is most obviously, though not exclusively, the case with the Work-Study programs and related programs of cooperative education and community service. An expectation that most students will earn a significant part of their educational expenses can also be an expectation that students will learn to relate the meeting of their own needs to the making of a contribution to the work place and the society it serves.

Institutional Health

The health of institutions of higher education is another goal with which the purposes of student aid need to be reconciled. As has often been pointed out, student aid has features that in some ways make it an excellent vehicle for the support of institutions. Such support is indirect, in that aid awards are made to students who then use them to pay their college bills. Need-based aid is made available to students on the basis of their characteristics, not on the basis of characteristics (other than cost) of the institutions they attend, so occasions for a coercive or even a "chilling" review of institutional programs are minimized. It is hard to think of a method for the large-scale public financing of higher education that is less intrusive and more consistent with institutional autonomy.

It has been argued, however, that the other side of accepting aid through students is to place the fate of educational programs in the fickle hands of students, who may make choices on the basis of misinformation or mere fad. The potential for mischief from this source appears, however, largely theoretical. The growth of student aid in recent years has not been accompanied by sudden, large changes in enrollment patterns attributable to this kind of behavior. Students often seem to have adjusted their expectations more realistically than institutions, as in the case of the decline of enrollments in teacher credential programs. The more sophisticated consultants who advise institutions on the recruitment of students warn that attempts to attract students on the basis of fads and gimmicks tend to fail.

More problematic is the possibility that some schemes of student aid could exacerbate a growing conflict between public and private institutions over public support. The declining size of the traditional college-age group and changing preferences about higher education and its timing have transformed a scarcity of college places into a surplus. Both old institutions with valued traditions and new ones with cherished aspirations feel threatened. The competition for students has begun in earnest

We believe that student aid should be even-handed in dealing with this competition. The student aid system can strengthen public institutions in their traditional mission of extending access to higher education without regard to the kinds of private affiliations that have played a large role in the development of constituencies for private higher education. At the same time, the student aid system can enable a large and strong private sector to continue to provide a diversity of programs and a standard of autonomy needed by higher education as a whole.

We urge that the controversy between public and private institutions over student aid be resolved in terms of principles of fair competition. By this we mean that:

- The distribution of student aid funds should not overwhelm the efforts of public and private institutions to compete in providing services to students.
- Students and their families should continue to be expected to pay more if they choose private institutions, but not unmanageably more.

Keeping the Commitments in Focus

The changing goals of student aid and the variety of interests at stake should not, we believe, be allowed to divert efforts to build a student aid system designed to make good on a national commitment to equality of opportunity for higher education. Now is the time to reinforce, not weaken, the need-based character of the aid system if it is to serve well needy students, the colleges and universities they attend, and the national welfare.

We urge the adoption of the proposals made in this report in order to make the emerging student aid system adequate to these goals and, at the same time, worthy of continued public trust and fair to students and institutions. Changes in the system will be necessary as conditions change. But an adequate program is now feasible within the budgetary resources available. What is required is effort and a statesmanship which looks to the national interest beyond narrow special interests.

References

American Bankers Association. *Bulletin No. 405.* Washington, D.C., 1978.

American Council on Education. *National Norms for Entering College Freshmen.* Washington, D.C., 1967-1973 (annual; see Cooperative Institutional Research Program for later years).

Astin, A. W. *Preventing Students from Dropping Out.* San Francisco: Jossey-Bass, 1975.

Atelsek, F. J., and Gomberg, I. L. *Student Assistance: Participants and Programs, 1974-75.* Washington, D.C.: American Council on Education, 1975.

Atelsek, F. J., and Gomberg, I. L. *Estimated Number of Student Aid Recipients 1976-77.* Higher Education Panel Reports, No. 36. Washington, D.C.: American Council on Education, 1977.

"Boyer Urges Truce Between Federal Government, Educational Community." *Higher Education Daily,* December 13, 1978, p. 2.

Breneman, D. W. "The Outlook for Student Finance." *Change,* October 1978, *10* (9), 48-49, 62.

Budget of the U.S. Government. Washington, D.C., 1976-1980 (annual).

Carnegie Commission on Higher Education. *Quality and Equality: Revised Recommendations—New Levels of Federal Responsibility for Higher Education.* New York: McGraw-Hill, 1970.

Carnegie Commission on Higher Education. *Higher Education: Who Pays? Who Benefits? Who Should Pay?* New York: McGraw-Hill, 1973.

Carnegie Council on Policy Studies in Higher Education. *The Federal Role in Postsecondary Education: Unfinished Business 1975-1980.* San Francisco: Jossey-Bass, 1975.

Carnegie Council on Policy Studies in Higher Education. *The States and Private Higher Education: Problems and Policies in a New Era.* San Francisco: Jossey-Bass, 1977.

The Carnegie Foundation for the Advancement of Teaching. *More Than Survival: Prospects for Higher Education in a Period of Uncertainty.* San Francisco: Jossey-Bass, 1975.

The Carnegie Foundation for the Advancement of Teaching. *The States and Higher Education: A Proud Past and a Vital Future.* San Francisco: Jossey-Bass, 1976.

"Conferees Deadlocked on BEOG Funding, Agree on Other Higher Ed Money." *Higher Education Daily*, October 5, 1978, pp. 1-4.

Congressional Budget Office. *Social Security Benefits for Students.* Washington, D.C., 1977.

Congressional Budget Office. *Federal Aid to Postsecondary Students: Tax Allowances and Alternative Subsidies.* Washington, D.C., 1978a.

Congressional Budget Office. *Federal Assistance for Postsecondary Education: Options for Fiscal Year 1979.* Washington, D.C., 1978b.

Cooperative Institutional Research Program, American Council on Education and University of California at Los Angeles. *National Norms for Entering College Freshmen.* Los Angeles, 1974-1978 (annual; see American Council on Education for earlier years).

Dresch, S. P. *Final Memorandum on Alternative Federal Loan Programs and Proposals.* New Haven, Conn.: Institute for Demographic and Economic Studies, 1978.

Esenwein, G. A., and Karr, J. "Median Income and the Tax Burden." Memorandum prepared for the House Education and Labor Committee. Washington, D.C.: Congressional Research Service, Library of Congress, May 9, 1978.

Fields, C. M. "The 1980 Budget: Basic Research Gains; Many Education Programs Fall Behind." *Chronicle of Higher Education*, January 29, 1979, pp. 3-4.

Food Stamp Act of 1977: Report on HR 7940 of the House of Representatives Committee on Agriculture. 95th Cong., 1st Sess. Washington, D.C.: U.S. Government Printing Office, 1977.

Freeman, R. B. *Black Elite: The New Market for Highly Educated Black Americans.* New York: McGraw-Hill, 1976.

Froomkin, J. *Middle-Income Students and the Cost of Postsecondary Education.* Washington, D.C.: Joseph Froomkin, 1978.

"GSL Needs Sallie Mae's Help to Strengthen Program, Renew Confidence." *Higher Education Daily*, June 15, 1978, p. 5.

Hansen, J. S. "The State Student Incentive Grant Program: An Assessment of the Record and Options for the Future." Report prepared for the Sloan Commission on Government and Higher Education. New York: College Entrance Examination Board, 1979.

Hansen, J. S., and Gladieux, L. E. *Middle-Income Students: A New Target for Federal Aid? Tax Credits and Student Assistance Programs.* New York: College Entrance Examination Board, 1978.

Hartman, R. W. "The National Bank Approach to Solutions." In L. D. Rice (Ed.), *Student Loans: Problems and Policy Alternatives.* New York: College Entrance Examination Board, 1977.

Hauptman, A. M. "Student Loan Defaults: Toward a Better Understanding of the Problem." In L. D. Rice (Ed.), *Student Loans: Problems and Policy Alternatives.* New York: College Entrance Examination Board, 1977.

"HEW Cleaning Up Aid Programs; More Initiatives on Way." *Higher Education Daily,* July 28, 1978, pp. 1-2.

"HEW to Extend Checks for GSL Defaulters to Military Personnel." *Higher Education Daily,* October 13, 1978, p. 4.

"House-Senate Conferees Agree on $2.6 Billion for BEOG." *Higher Education Daily,* October 10, 1978, pp. 1-2.

"Misguided Compassion Means Less Loans for Students, Says HEW Official." *Higher Education Daily,* December 15, 1978, pp. 5-6.

National Association of State Scholarship and Grant Programs. *10th Annual Survey: 1978-79 Academic Year.* Deerfield: Illinois State Scholarship Commission, 1978.

National Manpower Institute. *An Untapped Resource: Negotiated Tuition-Aid in the Private Sector.* Washington, D.C., 1978.

Nelson, J. E. "Are Parents Expected to Pay Too Much?" *The College Board Review,* Summer 1974, *92,* 11-15.

Nelson, J. E., and Van Dusen, W. D. "The Question of Affordability." New York: College Entrance Examination Board, 1978 (duplicated).

"OE Data Show 201 Schools with NDSL Default Rates Exceeding 50 percent." *Higher Education Daily,* March 16, 1978, p. 1.

Peng, S. S. "Trends in the Entry to Higher Education: 1961-1972." *Educational Researcher,* January 1977, pp. 15-19.

Poverty Amid Plenty. Report of the President's Commission on Income Maintenance Programs (Ben W. Heineman, Chairman). Washington, D.C., 1969.

President of the United States. *Economic Report of the President: Transmitted to the Congress, January 1978.* Washington, D.C.: U.S. Government Printing Office, 1978.

President of the United States. *Employment and Training Report of the President, 1978.* Washington, D.C.: U.S. Government Printing Office, 1978.

Report to the Congress of the Committee on Process of Determining Student Loan Special Allowances. Washington, D.C.: Student Loan Marketing Association, 1977.

Special Analyses, Budget of the U.S. Government. Washington, D.C., 1976-1980 (annual).

Spies, R. R. *The Effects of Rising Costs on College Choice.* New York: College Entrance Examination Board, 1978.

"State, Territories, and D.C. Will Spend $828 Million on Student Aid in 1978-79." *Chronicle of Higher Education,* November 27, 1978, p. 5.

Suchar, E. W., Ivens, S. H., and Jacobson, E. C. *Student Expenses at Postsecondary Institutions, 1978-79.* New York: College Entrance Examination Board, 1978.

U.S. Bureau of the Census. "Income in 1967 of Families in the United States." *Current Population Reports,* Series P-60, No. 59. Washington, D.C., 1969.

U.S. Bureau of the Census. "Estimates of the Population of the United States, by Age, Sex, and Race: 1970 to 1977." *Current Population Reports,* Series P-25, No. 721. Washington, D.C., 1978a.

U.S. Bureau of the Census. "Money Income and Poverty Status of Families in the United States: 1977." *Current Population Reports,* Series P-60, No. 116. Washington, D.C., 1978b.

U.S. Bureau of the Census. "Income of Families and Persons in the United States." *Current Population Reports,* Series P-60. Washington, D.C., annual.

U.S. Bureau of the Census. "School Enrollment—Social and Economic Characteristics of Students." *Current Population Reports,* Series P-20. Washington, D.C., annual.

U.S. National Center for Education Statistics. *Projections of Education Statistics.* Washington, D.C., annual.

U.S. National Center for Education Statistics. *Financial Statistics of Institutions of Higher Education: Fiscal Year 1976: State Data.* Washington, D.C., 1978a.

U.S. National Center for Education Statistics. *The Condition of Education, 1978 Edition.* Washington, D.C., 1978b.

U.S. Veterans Administration. *Veterans Benefits Under Current Educational Programs: Information Bulletin.* Washington, D.C., 1970-1978.

von Moltke, K., and Schneevoigt, N. *Educational Leaves for Employees: European Experience for American Consideration.* San Francisco: Jossey-Bass, 1977.

Wagner, A. P. "Comparing the Costs of Attendance and Available Financial Resources of 1977-78 College Students." Unpublished paper, Indiana University, November 1977.

Wenc, L. M. "The Role of Financial Aid in Attrition and Retention." *College Board Review,* Summer 1977, *104,* 17-21.

Woodhall, M. *Review of Student Support Schemes in Selected OECD Countries.* Paris: Organization for Economic Cooperation and Development, 1978.

Index

Academic deficiencies: and Basic Grants override, 9, 34; and part-time enrollment, 189
Access, concept of, 166
Admissions, standards of, and choice, 168
Adult students: aid for, 10; independent, 110; recommendations on, 55-56. *See also* Independent students; Part-time students
Affirmative action, and enrollment rates, 3
Aid to Families with Dependent Children, 98
Alabama, grant programs in, 212
Alaska, grant programs in, 212
American Bankers Association, 174*n*, 243
American College Testing (ACT) program, need analysis of, 80, 83-84. *See also* College Scholarship Service/ American College Testing schedule
American Council on Education, 76, 122*n*, 130*n*, 138*n*, 243
Arizona, grant programs in, 212
Arkansas, grant programs in, 212
Asian students, earnings of, 157*n*, 158*n*
Astin, A. W., 29, 124, 153, 243
Atelsek, F. J., 76, 105*n*, 106*n*, 109, 126*n*, 243
Attrition: and family income, 123; for financial reasons, 124. *See also* Persistence

Basic Grant program: amount given under, 69; background of, 69, 71-72; and calculating costs of adequate aid, 229, 230, 231, 232; and changing financial burden, 141*n*, 143, 147, 150; and choice, 169, 170; and coordination of aid, 208, 209-210, 211; defined, 63; duration of, limited, 43; and enroll-

ment rates, 3, 117, 118*n*, 119, 123; entitlement to, 90-91; and equality of opportunity, 8; fifty-percent-of-cost limitation of, 8, 14, 16-20, 35-36, 90; increase in, 33; and independent students, 30, 198-199; institutional impact of, 125, 126, 127, 128, 130, 132, 135-136, 137, 138-139; integrity and simplicity issues in, 220-221; and loan system, 184; and need analysis, 81, 84-86, 87-88; and need-based system, 162-164; and noninstructional costs, 14, 32; in Office of Education package, 10, 13; parental contribution schedule of, 38-43; and part-time students, 190-191; recipients of, 101, 102*n*, 103, 106, 107, 108-109, 111; under recommendations, 22; and self-help, 26; and social security benefits, 58-59; and State Student Incentive Grants, 47; ten percent override proposal for, 9, 10, 11, 13, 20, 28, 34, 41, 49, 190, 195, 198, 226; by type of institution, 24
Bellmon, H., 54*n*
Black institutions, student aid impact on, 132, 135, 136
Black men: earnings of, 155, 157, 158; enrollment rates of, 25, 113-114, 117-118, 120, 123
Black students: earnings of, 28; institutional choices by, 132, 137-138; work related to persistence among, 29
Black women: earnings of, 155, 157, 158, 159; enrollment rates of, 113-114, 117, 118, 121, 123
Breneman, D. W., 54, 243
Budget of the U.S. Government, 69*n*, 243

California: aid recipients in, 107; schol-